Caring vs Curing Embodied Engagement: I am not alone

Text copyright © 2016 remains with the authors and for the collection with ATF Press. All rights reserved. Except for any fair dealing permitted under the Copyright Act, no part of the publication may be reproduced by any means without prior permission. In- quiries should be made in the first instance with the publisher.

Ethics:
Volume 3, Number 2, 2016

Ethics: Contemporary Perspectives

We live in an evolving and increasingly complex global community and with this complexity comes a broad range of ethical issues. The new interdisciplinary journal, Ethics: Contemporary Perspectives, seeks to bring together scholars from across the humanities, social sciences, and sciences, including disciplines as diverse as philosophy, law, medicine and the study of world religions, to discuss these broad ethical issues in contemporary society. A peer reviewed journal, Ethics aimed at exploring our complex world, addressing both old and new ethical issues through scholarly discourse.

This is a new, international, interdisciplinary, and refereed journal which is to be published annually by ATF Press in association with the University of Adelaide Research Unit for the Study of Society, Law and Religion (RUSSLR). The publication is both an on- line and print edition journal. The first issue of the journal has an international line up of leading scholars in a range of disciplines from the USA, Canada, New Zealand, France and Australia. It will address the theme of 'The Ethics of Ethics' and will come out in the first half of 2013. The second edition in 2014 will deal with 'Space Ethics'.

Editor Board
Dr Bernadette Richards, Law School University of Adelaide, Editor in Chief.
Associate Professor Paul Babie, Director, Research Unit for the Study of Society, Law and Religion, University of Adelaide
Professor Robert Crotty, former Director, Ethics Centre of South Australia, Emeritus Professor of Religion and Education, University of South Australia

Business Manager
Mr Hilary Regan, Publisher, ATF Theology, PO Box 504 Hindmarsh, SA 5007, Australia. Fax +61 8 82235643.

Vol 3/ 2 2016

Subscription rates
Print:	Local: Individual Aus $55, Institutions Aus $65.
	Overseas: Individuals US $60, Institutions US $65.
OnLine:	Local: Individuals Aus $45, Institutions: Aus $55.
	Overseas: Individuals US $50, Institutions US $60
Print and Online	Local: Individuals Aus $65, Institutions Aus $85.
	Overseas: Individuals US $70, Institutions US $80.

Ethics: Contemporary Perspectives is published by ATF Press an imprint of the ATF Press Publishing Group which is owned by ATF (Australia) Ltd (ABN 90 116 359 963) and is published once a year. ISSN 2201-3563

Cover design by Astrid Sengkey. Text Minion Pro Size 11

Caring vs Curing
Embodied Engagement:
I am not alone

by Susan Bardy

Adelaide
2016

Introduction

This is the sequel to *Choosing End of Life Nursing*, the volume which familiarised the reader with my life and the developments in my nursing career and the gradual passion of caring for people in end of life situations.

In this work I wanted to succeed in understanding vocational ideations of palliative care nursing. For many months I played with the thought that I needed to find out why it was that I was so strongly attracted to the philosophy: why was it was that this was the one caring model I never tied of?

In this volume the personal journey joins with the broader culture of palliative care nursing by interviewing those who chose palliative care nursing and examine the reasons for changes in careers from acute, curing based nursing to palliative caring for those in end of life nursing.

Chapter One—*Celebrating by Sharing*—is the longest section of the study where I travel the world of palliative nursing with participant observers. It is about the actively working nurse and includes extensive analytical discussion of how I understand the sense of professional change, and the significance of beliefs for the reasoning behind vocational transformation. Here is where experienced palliative care nurses in interview situations join me. This is where we compare notes about our nursing practice and it is where I first meet the research findings.

Chapter Two—*Inner Secrets of Being There at the End of Life*—is where I spend time with interview transcripts and begin to give answers to how and why participants chose the nursing of terminally ill people.

Chapter Three—*Almost the End*—is the concluding discussion that addresses the heart of the research question and gives an answer to transformation of nursing ideals from a curing model to a caring only approach when death of the patient is inevitable.

The *Epilogue,* is where I write another letter this time to both of my sons and ask them to be there when my time comes for the end of life through a life limiting illness. I ask them to see that the palliative care professionals observe my final wishes.

Table of Contents

Introduction		iv
Chapter 1	Celebrating by Sharing	1
Chapter 2	Inner Secrets of Being There at the End of Life of the Other	49
Chapter 3	Almost the End	67
Epilogue	A final request	81
Bibiliography		83

Chapter 1
Celebrating by Sharing

In the previous volume I have mentioned how auto-ethnographic methodology does not necessarily specify contributions from 'others' as data, but does not discourage it either.[1] Chang maintains that in auto-ethnography the researchers' past and present is the primary source of data, but she acknowledges that interviewing others does play a role.[2] An example of this is Carolyn Ellis' interactive interview with Christine Kissinger and Lisa Tillman-Healy.[3] A dinner party conversation between the three introduced how the interviewer by contributing her story stimulated a spirited discussion about eating disorders. Laurel Richardson transcribed her interview with Louisa May in the form of a poem that described a painful life.[4] Chang again believes that collaborating in this manner could stir memories of personal experience that often becomes a valuable research finding. I could not help but agree with this as I muse over how I should introduce this section. Here I bring into focus stories of others, complementing my autobiographical account of nursing transformation.

A group of invited nurses joined me in describing how they came to work in the area of palliative care. These participants, in their independent way, added knowledge to complete the jigsaw

---

1.
2. H Chang, *Autoethnography As Method* (Walnut Creek, CA: Left Coast Press, Inc, 2008), 105-106.
3. C Ellis, C Kiesinger & L Tillman-Healy, 'Interactive interviewing: talking about emotional experience', in *Reflexivity and voice,* edited by R Hertz Sage Publications, Thousand Oaks, California, 1997).
4. Laurel Richardson, *Fields of Play: Constructing an Academic Life* (New Jersey: Rutgers University Press, New Brunswick, New Jersey, 2001).

of palliative caring. Since I was the one who invited them to share personal and professional stories I was responsible for their safety during the interviews. I envisaged the possibility of discussing intimate experiential stories that I would be trusted with, and as such I paid close attention to ethical aspects of interviewing. Participating nurses were each given written information about the project and asked to sign a document stating their agreement to be a part of the research. This they all did. I also committed to keeping their person anonymous by using pseudonyms throughout the writing of the interview transcript.

Encounters of a personal kind

During twenty years in palliative care nursing I not only observed patients' prognosis but also watched how other nurses undertook this work. On the whole my personal stories directed this study, but I also travelled the wider world of the palliative care culture in an auto-ethnographic style where I was the initial object and subject of the research.[5] To compliment this I invited peers in palliative care nursing to share their stories to be the source energy of my work in an attempt to unlock my understanding of what it is which is motivation for people to chose nursing those who are at the end of life.[6] With this let me I introduce the next research activity that for me was not only stimulating but added ethnographic relevance. I am referring to the interviews with invited nurses whose ten or more years of clinical experience in palliative care complemented the study. The knowledge gained from the interviews strengthened and supported the way I saw clinical practice in end of life nursing. Little did I realise at the time that sharing experiential stories with colleagues in a setting of unstructured interviewing contributed not only to my

---

5. Elligson, "'Then You Know How I Feel": Empathy, Identification, and Reflexivity in Fieldwork', *Qualitative Inquiry*, 4/4 (1988): 492–514; C Ellis, *The Ethnographic I'*, (Walnut Creek, Lanham, New York, Oxford: Alta Mira Press, 2004); A Kolker 'Thrown Overboard: The Human Cost of Health Care Rationing', in *Composing ethnography*, edited by C Ellis & A Bochner (Wlanut Creek, California: Alta Mira Press, 1996).
6. Chang, *Autoethnography As Method*, 106.

better understanding of palliative care but also reassured me of the appropriateness of my personal caring approach.[7]

Readers may well ask why a description of interview contents in the following section will not exclusively focus on the research question, and at the same time wonder why I consider the significance of the broader aspect of palliative care practice? My main argument is around the reason for nurses' transformation. At the same time however I am anxious to learn what it takes to travel from curing to caring in a nurse's career. My personal experience was of a slowly evolving change of my care outlook over time.

The next step, as it should be, is how I went about including other palliative care nurses in this auto-ethnographic storying experience.

Challenge of meeting the 'other'

Coming together in the interview environment, conducting face-to-face unstructured dialogues with nursing peers opened the door to a special interaction. What I want to begin this section with will reveal how I went about the actual 'doing' of the interviews. Of course, most of us imagine that we know how interviewing is done, However, auto-ethnography, as far as I understand it, assumes that the researcher will both explain why interviewing is appropriate as a data collecting tool to add to the self exposition of the researcher, and additionally explain how those interviews were conducted to complement the topic of the study. I mentioned in the previous volume that he methodology, as characterised by many practitioners, does not strictly prescribe interviewing others as data, but instead leaves to the researcher to show why it is justified in her case. Clinical nursing is a team activity and that is why I feel more comfortable with other nurses joining me in the discussion. Nurses in their clinical work setting invariably leave notes for each other, talk in person or in recorded messages—all these activities are appropriate tools to the trade. In addition, nurses

---

7. B Sherman-Heyl, 'Ethnographic interviewing', in *Handbook of Ethnography*, edited by P Atkinson, A Coffey, S Delamont, J Lofland & L Lofland (London: Sage Publications Ltd, 2002).
FJ Gubrium, & JA Holstein, editors 2001, *Handbook of Interview Research* (London: Sage Publications, 2001).

also feel comfortable talking with patients, in fact that is considered a major component of the job of nursing and more so of palliative care.

I had imagined that interviewing as such should not present a problem for me because it is a common feature of patient/nurse communication. On second thought I had to admit that really there were large differences between research interviewing and patient assessment. In my clinical role I would not interview in a formal sense but would analyse therapeutic information about the patient's physical wellbeing, information about their history and what brought on the hospital admission, etc. This was not an interview as such. Rather I would ask questions and be making an assessment to gain, as far as possible, a comprehensive picture of the patient, and their needs.

In my research interviews I was primarily interested in the participants palliative care practice and history. I aimed for a free-flowing interaction, where the responses would reflect on the main topic. Interestingly, when it came to meeting a peer, in a one to one intimate research situation, there was often a barely perceptible level of discomfort. This was by no means one sided because I believe both parties could feel somewhat intimidated. I must confess that I found it easier talking with a new patient than seeking out nurses for information about their professional expertise. With patients I was invited to share my nursing knowledge and help them, while with nurses in a formal 'interview' I was the one approaching them for information.

Before getting to the interview stage I had to find people who were willing to participate. I thought this would be the easy part and did not count on the emerging obstacles. Involvement with humans as research subjects requires ethics approval, and this was sought and approved by the relevant authorities. I published a letter in the Australian nurses journal inviting nurses to participate in the research. I interviewed a number of respondents, travelled to various parts of the country and met people in venues of their choice.

It was challenging—meeting strangers in motel rooms between conference presentations, private homes, in my own home and even in a noisy café. Yet this was nowhere as intimidating as actually walking up to a private home and wondering what I would find. An offer of a steaming mug of coffee, served by my host before starting the interview, soon relaxed us both. However no matter how anxious either side felt, I almost immediately found common ground for discussion. Perhaps I was lucky in the people I interviews, but, invariably, the interviews were not only an information or data gathering exercise but were the sharing between two like-minded spirits. I was made aware of my membership of an elite group of nurses whose way of life and professional experience encouraged the sharing of knowledge and the affinity with each other

My interviews followed an auto-ethnographic unstructured style, where the questions were open ended and were kept to a minimum. In fact these meetings were dialogical in nature, one where exchanges 'allow[ed] flexibility in questioning and responding' in the structure of personal stories in the culture of palliative care nursing.[8] Other genre specific characteristics such as border crossing, the blurring of vision between disciplines, use of self-examination and the fusing of individual horizons were also features of the discussions.[9] Telling of anecdotal stories of patient care added richness to the recall of difficult physical and emotional situations. Participants brought their personal unique style to pre interview chats. For instance a lunch with Rosalie in a beautiful garden setting and the company of birds and the three legged Kelpie (an Australian sheep dog), nearly made me forget that I was there to talk of death and dying. As it almost happened in Sue's comfortable lounge room where we had daughter Mara's company while we enjoyed coffee brewed by Sue's husband. We got into excited conversation about Mara's year 12 examinations and her chosen future in nursing.

Another time there was the meeting with three community nurses in an Australian country township that left me wishing I could stay and work with them.

---

8. Chang, *Autoethnography As Method*, 2008, 105.
9. Ellis, 'The ethnographic I' 2004; Chang, 2008 *Autoethnography As Method*, 2008; K Etherington, Etherington, K 2004, *Becoming a Reflexive Researcher* (Gateshead: Atheneum Press, 2004); E Foster, *Communicating at the End of Life: Finding Magic in the Mundane* (New York: Lawrence Erlbaum Associates, Publishers, 2007); J Wright, J 2008, 'Searching One's Self: The Autoethnography of a Nurse Teacher', *Journal of Research in Nursing*, 13/4 (2008): 338–347; Bartleet, 2009; BL Bartleet, 2009, 'Behind the Baton: Exploring Autoethnographic Writing in a Musical Context, *Journal of Contemporary Ethnography*, 38/6 (2009): 713–733.

Recording the interviews was the easy part. I used an old-fashioned tape recorder and then types them up after each interview. Transcribing the interviews had the advantage of promoting understanding of contextual meanings right from the start. The act of transcription according to Kvale is not only transferring the words from recording to paper but 'is in itself an interpretive process'.[10] In typing I was transported back to each meeting just by listening to the voices. I was rewarded with reliving each interview and getting the best possible picture of the visit. It was amazing how this promoted easier recognition and understanding of sensitivities and subtle nuances that I often discovered for the first time while listening the second time around. The importance of this emerged as I gradually realised that hearing the tapes over and over again recreated the mood of the settings and coloured the conversations. This was an introspective experience and prompted a 'dialogue with myself'[11] that clarified the meaning of the interview contents. I got deeply involved with each story and wished for nothing more than to remain there as long as possible, and that is what prompted me to transform transcripts into stories.

Knocking on Doors

Auto-ethnographic interviewing provides an opportunity to communicate with the 'outsider' or the one in the ethnographic landscape where 'conversing [is] a way [of] belonging, coping, caring and loving'.[12] The intention of the interview was to 'provide external data that gives contextual information to confirm, complement, or reject introspectively generated data'.[13] Interpretation or making sense of the interviews in this manner focuses on the storied contents of the meeting and encourages the interviewer to dip into personal ethnography and cultural experience to help understand the 'momentary, contingent meanings' that the process reveals.[14] Active

---

10. S Kvale, *InterViews* (London: Sage Publications, 1996), 160.
11. C Ellis, *Revision: Autoethnographic Reflections on Life and Work* (Walnut Creek, California: Left Coast Press, 2009).
12. A Bochner, 'Narrative Virtues', *Qualitative Inquiry*, 7/2 (2001): 131-158.
13. Chang, *Autoethnography As Method*, 104.
14. Bochner, 'Narrative Virtues', 140.

listening puts the interviewer into a complex psychological position where personal reflectivity can alter the meaning of the significant points, but an open-minded interviewer rarely speaks for the 'other' or the one being interviewed[15] and as such my transcriptions mirror what the interviewee said.

Conducting a one-on-one meeting in the auto-ethnographic context is more a conversation than an interview. It is a share and share alike bonding that produces meaning and emotional dynamics as we tune into the interactive communication.[16] The interviews started with a comfortable beginning and invariably this continued onto the formal activity that was a discussion of information; by sharing experiential stories qualifying the nurses I interviewed for the role of co-researchers.

Interviewees as co-researchers—why?

The auto-ethnographic interview method promoted the use of dialogue not set questioning, that allowed me to examine my 'subjectivity' in a relaxed and informal climate.[17] In a interview which is dialogical both researcher and participant are on equal footing, and both are fully informed of the nature of the research. 'Dialogic research dispenses with researchers and subjects, [participants]' says Colaizzi.[18] Here the researcher works in co-operation with the informant who then becomes the co-researcher. Dialogue develops into a 'situation of trust' that brings about the co-researcher's comfort with sharing existential dimensions.

The interviews I conducted with palliative care peers put me in a position where I could safely disclose information concerning the research. There was never a time when I had to withhold my purpose and as such co-researchers were on an equal plane with me and trusted me as I trusted them.

---

15. M Gordon, 'Listening as Embracing the Other: Martin Buber's Philosophy of Dialogue', *Educational Theory*, 61/2 (2011): 207–219.
16. Ellis, *'The ethnographic I'*.
17. Chang, *Autoethnography As Method*, 103.
18. PF Colazzi, 'Psychological Research as the Phenomenologist Views it', in *Existential-phenomenological Alternatives for Psychology*, edited by RS Valle & M King, (New York: Oxford University Press, 1978), 69.

Storytellers: some personal data

The group was predominantly female. The women were without exception bedside carers, while the two males had involvement with organisational and educational matters at the time of the interviews. Ages varied from thirty to sixty years, with two participants only being in their early thirties. They were all experienced palliative care nurses with an average length of time in this specialty being six years. Most had some years in medical and surgical experience before transferring to palliative care. Most of this group remained with the organisation they commenced their palliative care work with for up to fifteen years of service. This did seem to indicate a degree of job satisfaction. But, this service length will be discussed later. The diverse palliative care settings included institutional hospice nursing, community district care, nurse education and one male participant was a full time PhD candidate at the time.

Writing the other and thinking the self

My co-researchers on their home turf opened up and told me what mattered to them most in palliative care opening my awareness to how similar we were in the approach to our professional role. While writing the 'other' I suddenly discovered that I am also writing 'myself'. Tales told by 'others' often embodied my experience of day-to-day practice.

Dynamics of the written word

Evaluating the interview contents is a journey of discovery. It begins with how and where the co-researchers and I met, initial reactions to the people, to their physical mannerism, to the feel for their humanity. Sitting and exchanging stories is the easy part; making sense of what I heard is another story.[19] In my head and heart I have a collection of shared lives that I treasure. They are in the character of narratives by a group of generous people who thought that by telling of their experience they would open other hearts and minds to the awareness of human goodness. Strolling into the gardens and homes

---

19. Ellis, *The ethnographic I*, 58–85.

of the people I met for the first time, and experiencing the face-to-face encounter was not only physical but also emotional. Surprisingly I was generally at ease because once I got the conversation going I could not help but be the 'constant nurse' in the company of those who unlike me were still active at the bedside.

During the interviews the only time I felt any level of discomfort was when I had to face a nurse I still worked with on a day to day basis. My reflection on this experience is as follows:

> *Seeing someone almost daily, exchanging professional nursing talk, then sitting down with that person in the role of a researcher made me feel uneasy. I never thought of this possibility before as work colleagues were usually rather keen to be interviewed and I assumed we would be comfortable with the changed roles. I noted the tension for the first time with Beth. We knew each other well as colleagues but we did not socialise outside working hours. So here we were in a one on one situation embarking on an academic discourse addressing personal issues. Beth's obvious nervousness did not add to my confidence, but I decided to see this encounter as a learning process, and I did value her participation. Turning on my best observational skills, I listened, and it worked.*

On returning to the transcripts I again found Art Bochner to be my wise mentor when I heard him reassure me that in the 'dialectical space of agony and pleasure, agony is born of the inadequacies of language'.[20] Yes, it is difficult to explain an experience 'of living a life and the smoothing orderliness we bring to it when we write'. I can still hear the voices of nurses I met in 2006, but how could I describe them in writing when I have to be smooth and orderly. Can I trust my memory, can I depend on it for accuracy now, years later when it may now be my 'response to what inspires my recollection'.[21] I cannot help if things I learnt in the ensuing years may colour my reminiscences somewhat. What was told to me then has not changed, but by seeing it in a more experienced light I could understand it differently.

Once I completed transcribing the spoken word into writing I sent a copy to each of the co-researchers to authenticate the transcript. All

---

20. Bochner, 'Narrative Virtues', 197.
21. Bochner, 'Narrative Virtues', 198.

agreed with the accuracy of the transcribed work, and that gave me leave to proceed with the research writing.

The Interviews

Almost a confession—trust and communication

Time spent in listening to and writing about co-researchers reminded me of how each encounter developed into a casually comfortable communication. The meetings were literally a celebration of being together in a climate of the new dawn of my palliative care. I listened and interacted with stories of amazing nursing experience where all storytellers had a generous spirit and willingly shared whatever they could about their life in caring for terminally ill people.

Each interview, with its individually unique thrust, had a distinctive quality not only because of where we met but also because of the individual way each of the nurses had a personal story to tell. There was, however, one whose account held much of what I believe encapsulated what I was looking for in my question about palliative care nursing. Rosalie's story illustrated the beginning of a professional life and gave a clear picture of a mid life career transformation. Rosalie's main concerns were around putting the welfare of her patients first in improving health or the end of life. The rationale for presenting the complete interview here in the form of a narrative is twofold. First, it demonstrates my technique in collecting data from the culture that I am researching and second, it indicates the way the personal stories most appropriately sit within my methodology. I transcribed each recorded interview practically verbatim; later translating them into detailed narratives.

Rosalie—first among equals

Rosalie's interview narrative serves a double purpose—one being a wish to show the style I use to narrate the interview transcripts, and the other to give an example of the nurse whose story best describes a career path from general nursing to hospice work.

Rosalie lived in one of those delightful small places in the Australian countryside where people go to have a break or get married in the old 'Abbey' a lovely converted convent where not only weddings but also other similar functions were held. I took a bus ride to get there and enjoyed the cool air conditioning on the coach after the long spell of hot weather in the city. I checked in to my hotel and waited to meet her.

A woman approached, dressed casually in jeans and a loose shirt. In the comfort of a sleek new car Rosalie introduced Sally her French Poodle. We chatted about the welcome rain that they had there a few days ago, making the grass greener and the flowers brighter. The car pulled up outside a small cottage among trees and a luscious garden, to the friendly greeting of a three-legged Australian kelpie dog.

'We will have lunch first', Rosalie said, as we entered the house. There was no doubt this was the home of a woman. It felt warm and had a casual elegance with cushions and rugs on the floor, a vase of roses and a table set for a feast. There was a 'feel good' atmosphere about it. We toasted the meeting with a glass of white wine and followed it with tasty morsels of cheese, a salad, fruit, nuts and an apple pie. Birds were singing and the sun was brilliant. Rosalie's two precious cats were stretching on the grass and the kelpie jumped around in his three-legged fashion. I almost forgot that this was supposed to be preliminaries to an interview about death and dying.

Sharing life experience was so easy in this lovely garden setting and I took a little longer to settle into the business of the research. Yet just being there was part of the research, because in this interaction I was learning so much about Rosalie. Eventually out came the recorder and I began the formal part of the interview by asking where nursing as a life commitment started for Rosalie.

Desire to be independent

Rosalie smiled as she answered. 'I was born in England. Nursing was far from my mind as a seventeen year old. Living in the country made me long for the 'big time' and I was very keen to get away from home.'

To take up studies in teaching would surely get her into the city so she applied for entry into that program. In her haste Rosalie forgot that she might be questioned about her reasons for choosing teaching as a future career and was surprised when she spotted the question on the application form asking, 'What do you want to teach?' The only subject coming to mind on the spur of the moment was geography, a subject she was not very good in. When her O level results [university entrance exam in Britain] came out Rosalie found that the only subject she failed was geography. So it was goodbye to teaching.

The next best course she thought, one that would surely get her away from country life, was nursing. 'Yes, the road to freedom will be legitimate and London here I come', she said to herself. At the nursing interview she told a few 'fairy tales' about her mother being a nurse, how it was in her genes and that her aunt was also a nurse as well. To her surprise she was accepted at the University College London. Wonderful, Rosalie thought, it is not that far from home and if things turn out for the worst 'I could always come back home to mother, she would not mind'. She was seventeen and a half and the world was hers. She was at last independent. Then she woke up!

The real world

According to Rosalie, starting nursing was the most traumatic thing that ever happened to her. She was petrified of the world that she was so unwise about and had to face head on. She had no concept of what she would be required to do as a new student nurse. The responsibility that a nursing career was sending her way was huge. Patients in the first ward were indeed very sick. As early as six months into her training she was sent to a busy children's hospital where little people were dying of cancer and as a seventeen-year-old Rosalie had to cope with masses of sadness as she remembered:

> *I found it very, very difficult and I remember it well. This would have been my second ward placement, and it was a neurological area, I looked after a young student nurse, she was diagnosed with a brain tumour. I actually was so traumatised by this that I started to get symptoms of a brain tumour myself, had the pins and needles in my arms and hands. I went to see the neurologist who did not say in so many words but more or less indicated that I was affected by the experience. It was all in my mind.*

Rosalie was responsible for people younger than herself in that second placement, and the majority of them were dying. Being on 'night duty' was the most stressful. As a nurse, when she had a chance to sit down, was at a dimly lit desk where staying awake and alert was not easy. Patients suffered more during the night. Darkness invariably brought up a dread of the future and dying. She was practically on her own with little support from experienced nurses. As I listened I could visualize that busy ward where seriously ill patients, like the eleven-year old Australian girl Elizabeth, lay awake, wanting a shoulder to cry on in the middle of the night:

> *Elizabeth suffered from a degenerative bone cancer to such an extent that her spine was disintegrating. She was in a head to waist plaster cast because if she had not been in the cast her spine would have just crumbled, She was dying. She used to talk to me during the night. I remember I was only eighteen and I would sit and talk with her whenever I had a minute. After I moved on to another ward she died about three months later. People like Elizabeth were the ones whom I will never forget.*

For Rosalie this early experience drafted the image of the ideal nurse. She was a grand storyteller about herself, the young woman who really wanted to be a teacher, the one who went on to save lives and comfort dying people.

A career path of gradual transformation

A nursing career in the early 1970s offered a rather restricted range of future opportunities for further studies. The nurse could become a midwife or opt for psychiatric nursing. Rosalie chose midwifery:

> *The part that drew me [to midwifery] was the sick babies and I did the special care baby ward and found that very rewarding. These children were so very, very handicapped. Where I actually did my midwifery we got some very sick babies and I found that I got a lot out of seeing the parents through the grief of [having] a handicapped child or the grief of losing one, and that's what drew me. And the other I was interested in was delivering a baby or looking after the mums. I was most interested in sick children though, the little tiny ones and their parents.*

So what is Rosalie telling me when she speaks of sick babies, disabled newborn babies, and parents facing inevitable grief? Rosalie made it clear that traumatic and difficult situations when a shoulder to cry on was called for, when death and grief were an issue, gave her the best job satisfaction. She thrived on helping the sad, lonely and disadvantaged people. Yet now the 'essential Rosalie' was ready for a new challenge. She has not lost that seventeen-year-old girl's enthusiasm for the next adventure.

What could be the most exciting step for a girl to take but travel the world! Going to Australia to join her twin brother 'sounded like the best adventure I could imagine' thought Rosalie as she fed the next premature baby and wiped the tears of another mother's face who just lost her newborn.

Travelling to the other end of the world was about as challenging as it could get.

'Stop Rosalie', she told herself, 'every nurse is a midwife these days. Will you find it easy to get a job with only two certificates?'

Being practical she decided to find the best way to ensure her future.

Another certificate—another adventure

An added qualification for the travelling nurse could increase employment opportunities. An Intensive Care (ICU) certificate would surely impress a potential employer! Thus Rosalie left the comfort of mothers and babies only to front up to a complex technology laden world. She had to admit that the environment of the intensive care unit sent shivers up and down her spine, and sent her back to being 'scared', like she was with dying children when she was only seventeen:

> By that time I was nursing for twelve years but had never worked in intensive care. That took me right back to my student days absolute fear of another difficult situation. I was back there again. I have never done this care with all the machines. I was very, very frightened. And then again it came to me [as at age seventeen] I might be frightened but I don't want that the person I am looking after to be frightened also. Patients in intensive care were there often after major surgery and when coming around [waking up] on no account were they to be frightened.

Rosalie was still the girl from long ago. She demonstrated a way of overcoming personal difficulties in the face of tragedy. A disastrous incident usually brought out the best in her. Overcoming her fear she learnt to manage high technology and to love her patients in Intensive Care:

> *I really loved looking after people who were in a crisis situation. They came to us because they had a really serious difficult event or what ever. And the interesting thing I found about ICU patients that once they wound up in intensive care they would never be the same again. It is like a grief thing that they went through. Whether it is a major heart attack or a brain infarct or some trauma that was quite life changing and the family went through it also and even if the patient recovered, things would never be the same.*

In the 1970s Intensive Care was the new 'glamour certificate', and jobs were easy to find with the qualification she had. Rosalie found employment with the first Australian hospital she approached. She found the nurses in the unit very skilled and 'up to date' with all the technology, but she had discomfort with the patient selection criteria:

> *What I did find, and it overwhelmed me, was that patients we looked after were very sick, they were often terminally ill and I was looking after people who were dying or trying to die . . . that worried me a lot. I was quite frustrated and I was very sad.*

Rosalie spoke softly as if searching for words, not wanting to offend yet wanting to be honest, and I had to agree with her feelings:

> *Because working in that environment for the nurses it was a failure when somebody died. 'We can't have that, when they are here, we must be seen to be doing something' was the key to critical care. And I found that really sad because I was quite comfortable with the idea that some people had to die. I was very comfortable with the idea of talking the family through it. Invariably members of the family knew the score and often were very confused when they have to work it out for themselves.*

Disillusioned with saving lives at all cost

Rosalie had real understanding for terminally ill patients. She saw the frustration in families when asked to accept active treatment on behalf of the patient and were given hope when there was none. In the ICU, like with the sick children in her younger days she had appreciation for the value of listening when grief was the problem. She was ready to provide an understanding ear and a shoulder to cry on and was gentle when explaining the truth.

This rang bells for me too. I recalled how in critical care I watched almost dead patients being actively resuscitated. I remembered the night when a young nurse I worked with stood still at the bedside of an elderly man whose doctors could not agree on a way to tell the family that their father was dying. When the inevitable happened and the old man had a cardiac arrest the young registered nurse could not bring herself to begin resuscitation, while tears were running down her face. I have always remembered the face of that young woman even though I do not remember her name. So, I agreed with what Rosalie said next:

> *Lots of the patients I felt were not in the right place. Colleagues used to call me 'the death queen' because I would be very much inclined to look after people whom I felt were dying; they [other nurses] were very worried to look after the dying patient. I was happy to do it. Intensive Care nurses shied away from death because they saw it as failing, I never did. And I guess I had worked in intensive care long enough by then to recognise that a lot of people in that area got a buzz out of a patient's cardiac arrest. Proudly sharing how they got 'him back' being the operative term for a successful resuscitation. I used to find that running on adrenaline was not me.*

She stopped for a minute, looked at me:

> *I used to stand back and watch the situation and say what am I doing here? I don't know what we are all doing. I did not want to be a part of it and came to the decision that there must be a better way to die than this.*

Where to now?

Rosalie remembered other patients from the past, the ones who often were forgotten, those in the side rooms, not in the big bay with the other patients, for whom there was 'no more to be done' because the cure had 'failed'. She often saw physicians as they shook their heads and gave up. Rosalie thought back to her student days when she was comfortable with terminal illness, in the oncology ward of her younger days, when she gave sherry to her patients whose nausea then magically disappeared. I look back at that day in Rosalie's garden and recall how often she mentioned her student days during that interview. I sensed that Rosalie's wish to nurse terminally ill people stemmed from those first six months with the dying children when she was a teenager herself. Later when she followed a different path in obstetrics she still gravitated towards people in grief situations such as when she was with parents experiencing foetal deaths, a miscarriage or the birth of a deformed baby. She had an affinity to be with loss, with people who are never cured of a terminal illness, and being with suffering humanity who needed that extra mile of care as they came to the end of life.

I am not happy

It is difficult to feel unsettled in a job especially a nursing job when there is no work satisfaction, but only a level of distress. You know what you want and at the same time are in a bind to remain there. You think you cannot put your hand on your heart and say 'I have had enough'.

This was Rosalie in the Intensive Care Unit as she searched for a world where she could make a difference. The meeting with Mandy, a hospice nurse she had known for sometime, happened just at the right time. 'Why don't you call into the hospice one day?', Mandy suggested. Rosalie was truly desperate for a change and visited the hospice the following week:

> *It was interesting when I actually went there I found the layout to be quite different to how I imagined a hospice to be. The unit was on the first and second floors of the building. There was no garden. The nurse manager, a Scottish woman, was just*

> *beautiful and kind of embraced me not physically at first. She introduced me to everybody, the porter, the cleaner whoever was there, and every patient we saw she had a kind word for. I started work in that hospice soon after the visit and I never looked back. It was the most rewarding area of nursing I ever worked in. I have been there about thirteen years now and still thrive on it. I really thrive on that work.*

Rosalie's words were not meant for the benefit of the interview only. I sensed the passion behind the words. She believed in what she was saying, 'It was the most rewarding area of nursing I ever worked in'. Statements like this usually come straight from the heart.

Vocation

Rosalie's vocation stemmed from her early nursing days when as young as she was she did not turn away from pain, suffering and death. She was equally comfortable with Elizabeth the child in the plaster as she was later with parents of sick and dying babies. Yet had second thoughts when it came to people who were not allowed to die.

Recognition and acceptance when death needs to happen brought me to palliative care also, and seeing my mother's care in a hospice encouraged my decision to transfer to palliative care. I loved the spirit and the peace that met me as I crossed the threshold of the hospice, much like Rosalie whose reaction was identical to mine on her visit to the hospice where she still worked thirteen years later, at the time of the interview.

Her response to my next question of how she coped with people's curiosity about her chosen professional role did not surprise me:

> *When you are out socially people often ask what you do. This generally needs to be clarified, as people are interested in the area you work in. Palliative Care often gets a puzzled look. 'What does that mean?' The answer of 'you look after people at the end stage of their disease' prompts another question—'are they going to die?' I say 'Well usually they do die eventually'. The next question usually is, 'how can you work there?' My answer will always be that it is the most rewarding nursing I have ever done. 'It must be so sad,' people say. I reply in the affirmative. It is sad but it is also funny. There is a lot of humour. It is real and it is where we all are . . . I don't mean to talk clichés . . . but it is*

> *a gift for me to work there. There is this sick human being and a family and there is something very special when they let you walk with them.*

We not only shared stories about our patients, but we also talked about collegiality. It is important in hospice work to be comfortable with your co-workers. Rosalie as the senior nurse had the experience to mentor and support junior staff. She sorts out her personal issues first and then helps her colleagues:

> *I think with experience I find that when I have something traumatic at work I try and leave it there. I try and deal with it at work. I can honestly say I don't find that I get overwhelmed with somebody dying or situation with their families because personally I get so much out of dealing with it, no matter how involved. What I have grief with is when others [nurses] don't cope with their own issues and let patients and nurses feel it. That worries me.*

Workplace politics can be a problem. I sensed that Rosalie's personality and spirituality made her one to whom others are drawn. However what frustrated her most was when nurses occasionally talk about 'difficult patients' in a manner that lacks understanding for human suffering, pain and fear that manifests in difficult behaviour. There are times however when it is not so easy to put up with the rare personal abuse by a patient, no matter how sick they may be.

Not so academic 'nursing talk'

Rosalie: 'This has been so great because we talked about everything under the sun.' This spontaneous comment from Rosalie lifted the pace of a slowing interview. The discussion reached a point when we were no longer strangers. We wanted nothing more than to end this meeting by sharing our core values. And that was when scholarly talk became 'nurse talk'.

Time had flown, I note while taking a furtive glance at my watch. We have not even touched on the 'hands on nurse' doing the 'dirty nursing'. It was an aspect of my practice that I valued highly. Patients openly admitted to a fear of dying while I washed a sweaty body and cleaned a soiled bed. Most open discussions happened during down to earth physical care of those I looked after. As soon as I mentioned this Rosalie became animated and remembered:

> Yes, that is when you get to know the patient. They talk about their life. They tell you everything. It is very rich. You listen and talk with them, show them you are interested. You go on asking yourself; how was that, what did you do then? Because we want to know as we go on, we want to learn to care better.

The nurse in me listened to Rosalie talking about 'being there'. I was also 'there' for fifty years, washing patients, cleaning beds and having invaluable memories. I still miss it and always felt this same pain when during the interviews nurses talk about their work. It adds richness to the story even as it makes me sad. I am sad because patient care is no longer my life. It left an empty space.

We began to get tired. The sun slowly sank below the horizon, the birds quietly sat in the trees ready for the night, and it was time to call it a day. We had shared a great deal today. Rosalie had been such a pleasant hostess. Her story has a lot of 'me' in it but I do not apologise for that. Rosalie and I were very similar in our sensitivities to the professional role of the palliative care nurse. We were both aware of how dying people feel and understand that the ability to do death work is a special gift not given to many.

Rosalie – a final word from the palliative care nurse

> I think we palliative care nurses embrace the idea of life, and we are very much aware that life is going to end and that is real. You touch, you listen, and you are gentle, you do that little extra. When we talk about other areas of nursing or even every day life and say that life is going to end, we know the implication of that. It makes us feel that we know how any interaction with people we have is special. You do not just come upon people ad hoc or by chance I do not think, and you make the most of that interaction wherever you are.

The issues raised by Rosalie sounded familiar. Much of what she experienced was very similar to the stories of others.

Individual voice of the palliative practitioner

Palliative care is offered to seriously ill people in various venues as my informants mentioned earlier. It could be in an institutional setting where nursing and medical care is a twenty-four hour service such as in a hospice. In Australia hospice care is given in a hospital-like location for patients who cannot be managed at home, or who need observation during symptom management. Home palliative care in Australia was not as popularly accepted as in other countries, for example as in the United States, however it is gaining recognition here more so of late. One reason could be the increased availability of better support services for home nursing and increased preference by patients to die in a familiar atmosphere with their nearest and dearest at home.

Interview transcripts show convincingly that co-researchers followed two distinctly different paths when choosing where they were to work. Some preferred the institutional model while others opted for community palliative care that became available gradually. Nurses were comfortable with their choice, though those in the community were more forth coming about liking their preference.

Institutional palliative care—five voices

In this section I share the narrative of five interviews with nurses whose preference was bedside care. As I mentioned earlier the interviews were interactive and as such we shared more personal data about each other than qualitative interviews generally tend to do. This research plays out its concerns in a compassionate narrative style where all participants are openly co-operative and frank in their communication.

Mary—from intensive care to hospice

Mary chose haematological oncology for her first job as a registered nurse in the late 1980s. She committed to a forward-looking professional life. She chose to be in the Intensive Care Unit [ICU], like so many young nurses did at the time. The young fresh mind wanted challenges. Saving life was what nurses were created for–as she knew it at the time. Mary was impressed by the hustle and bustle of blood malignancies in a complex problem area full of very sick people. Patients were all actively treated in the hope of a cure, a long remission or just to live an extra few months, weeks or days. Mary really loved the work. The adrenalin rush of this busy place gave her a lot of pleasure. She settled there and got rather clever at managing difficult situations until her unit manager, an older nurse, took her aside and explained some important facts to remember about these people who were nursed behind high technology.

> *She taught me a lot about stepping back and seeing the person behind the technology. They are the important ones, the vulnerable people.*

And that is when it happened. Mary woke up to the reality of the situation. She consciously willed herself to stop and remember that people needed more than an over medicalised involvement in their illness management. There was another side to some of these desperately ill patients that no technological intervention could ever solve. The suffering was real, the pain was real, but the treatment often appeared as if it was out of a science fiction story where no one stops to see the humanity of those in the beds:

> *The doctors used to go and break the news of a devastating diagnosis to the patient, 'you've got leukaemia' and walk out again. You the nurse had to go in and pick up the pieces. I think I learnt a lot about talking with people after this and I also stopped and listened to what they had to say. The feeling of empathy came; I suddenly got empathy that I did not have before. If you are a kid you just . . . you just don't know.*

Mary, without even recognising it, had empathy way back in the side rooms of her training days, for those lonely dying patients there. I pointed this out to her while she unburdened herself about the cancer that was often coldly managed by the medical staff. She became restless as she looked around the busy unit with all its whizzing and beeping hardware and understood regretfully that suffering humanity under her vigilant care was treated as a disease, and not as a whole person. This was something that touched her deeply:

> *They [medical staff] can't step back and say that there is nothing more they can do. They say: 'but there is still one more thing we could try' [was the usual medical mantra]. And I sort of watched that and I used to get really frustrated that these people were not allowed to die, not allowed to die with dignity. Give them time to go home, get things in order, to talk to the family to just accept where they are going instead of making them think they are going to live.*

Mary eventually had had enough and transferred to a hospice nearby. That is how Mary's palliative care career started. She had a lot to learn, and admitted that at the time she was the 'high-powered oncology nurse', and needed to step back, slow down, to take time to look and listen.

I continued listening to Mary with interest. She spoke about her developing palliative care skills that told of patients dying with greater ease, less tragically, more comfortably and how it was so different with each given situation. I remembered this from my own experience with difficult deaths. Mary spoke softly, barely audible at times. Body language and facial expression indicated both sadness and joy almost at the same time:

> *I feel very privileged to be present with a family member when a loved one dies. You are sharing something with them something they cannot talk to most people about, something personal, and that is special.*

I felt comfortable when I asked Mary for her definition of a good death. The ultimate acceptance of death and dying, as far as I am concerned, is when a person can freely talk about the topic. Mary at the time of the interview had been a hospice nurse for a number of years so I expected an answer that was more than acceptable. I was not disappointed:

> *I think a good death is when all parties come together and the patient is peaceful as well as the family. When they all come to accept and are at peace with the death, even when the pain is not fully controlled. We can't always control all pain, but if everybody is at peace they [the dying people] can go quietly. And I think that is when we realize that if we can get them to a*

> *place where everyone is at peace with what is happening ... that could be good death.*

We could not leave it at this. There was an urgency to talk about death and dying. This was a good example of how a nurse evolves a hospice care personality and I encouraged Mary to go on because I felt she wanted to share things she had learnt at the bedside of dying patients. The strength people summoned up in the final days of life, the braveness of families in the adversity of loss:

> *Listening to some of these people, their strength is just amazing, their inner strength. Sometimes they gave me strength. It makes one look at life differently and you don't sweat the small stuff. It is hard to put into words. You know I am astounded at the way some people are so accepting of some awful things that are happening to them and are at peace with what is going on around and to them: they organise, they can talk to their families, keep them at ease and I am astounded how people plan funerals and things before they die. I don't know if I could do that. I don't know if I would be strong enough to do that.*

This quiet monologue by Mary opened memories of human existential strength in the face of heartbreak that invariably taught the hospice nurse emotional endurance. Yet there were days when it was just too much to bear. Mary was reminded of the helping hand of John a colleague, on a particularly difficult day when she was quite distressed after several deaths

> *John told me about the book of memories. He said remember your patient as a single book in a library. Every now and then you go to the bookshelf, pull a book down, you open it up. You can read it and you can laugh a bit, cry a bit, then close the book and put it back on the shelf. You have to close them tightly. Some don't close evenly and some could sit there for a long time and you just have to work through it, they are the hard ones. This helped me over the years. I still have an open book of a young woman whose father brought me a photo bookmark that is there with her metaphoric book of memories and I often look at her.*

Mary was a hospice colleague for some years at the time of this interview. I was interested that at her relatively youthful age of thirty-five years and why she remained in the hospice without the drive for a promotional role elsewhere. What is it that keeps her coming back to a demanding task day after day? Her answer was very simple:

> *It is hard to put it into words. I never ever not want to go to work, it is difficult to get out of bed in the morning, but I am glad to come to work. I am never tired of hospice work. It gives me joy, helping patients is what I like.*

I have known Mary since her student days. She impressed me even then with her patient care. Working with her in the hospice however raised my appreciation for her gentle nursing approach on another level. She impressed me with this modest admission of her hospice work. I cannot remember any nurse ever describing work ideals in quite the same words.

As I listened I came to the conclusion that Mary and I were very similar in our vocational ideals in a difficult to manage nursing arena. We both agree on being basic nurses but I question Mary's insistence on being an ordinary nurse—even as I always maintained that I was ordinary myself. There was a feeling about her that indicated peace, understanding and a special spirituality. She acknowledged human values and frailties and accepted them. Her work was her love made visible.

Beth—coming from intensive care

Beth, like Mary, was also disillusioned with workings in the Intensive Care Unit (ICU). Her story differed from that of Mary's because the time gap between ICU and hospice was much longer. After qualifying in general nursing and post graduate intensive care Beth married, moved to a small country town, and faced the cancer diagnosis of her eighteen-year-old brother. Soon after this her father died, also with cancer. She was involved in her brother's care by taking him to radiation therapy and sat with her father as he was dying .Yet through all this she never forgot certain distressing experience, in the ICU that left her scarred.

Beth sat quietly for a few minutes, and then picked up on her memories of deaths that were not managed well in the ICU. One that caused her particular angst was when ICU nurses while re-inserting a dislodged breathing tube failed to listen to the young patient's plea 'Please tell me am I dying?' It was common knowledge in the unit that young Jim was indeed dying yet the nurses did not find time to stop to console him after reinserting the tracheostomy tube. They concentrated on the futile life saving exercise and ignored his status as a human being. Jim was scared and no one spoke to him about his future. He wanted to know how long he had got, a question all dying people ask. Fair enough, the nurses concentrated on saving his life but for what, it would have been more respectful to talk about his future. The nurses forgot to reassure him that they cared and heard his plea. There was no chance later for explanations because Jim died that night.

Then there was the elderly man whose life support was switched off by the physician without first warning Beth about it. She best tells this herself:

> I arrived at the unit and took over my patient from the night nurse. One of the nursing tasks with a respirator patient was to do and record full vital sign observations every fifteen minutes. I then dusted the area. I cleaned everything, dusted everything and then did another set of observations. The doctor walked into the room and turned off the respirator as soon as I finished. He then brought the relatives in who sat next to this old man who was nearly dead. I was so upset as I went to the next patient, I was so angry. No one had told me that they were going to turn his respirator off. If I had known I would have shaved him. I would have used my fifteen minutes between observations to shave him. The family saw him unshaven. The last memory will be of his unkempt face.

My heart went out to Beth as she described this experience because at the time this happened she was a newly graduated registered nurse with little experience of death and dying. Yet she sensed the impropriety of this action. She was feeling deeply for the family's pain.

Later in midlife after gaining additional clinical skills she not only became a hospice nurse but also was responsible for setting up a rural Palliative Care Service. Even though she spoke easily about this she still stopped repeatedly and looked for the right word to describe her appreciation of palliative care. Beth wanted to open her heart and pay tribute to a nursing practice that gave her fulfilment in her role as a hospice nurse.

My own memory of being with terminally ill people and their families at the time of death brought into focus moments when I felt privileged to witness special relationships at a difficult time. I often wondered how I deserved being there when private grief was the issue and I felt like stepping back. Beth described how this was for her, and she did not mince her words:

> *I didn't know how good nursing in hospice was before I started palliative care. I did not know that I was going to meet the most amazing patients because in hospice the patients drop their façade. When they are in palliative care they drop all the crap. I had the privilege of meeting real people. It [palliative care] is very much better than any other nursing.*

I sensed Beth's tension around articulating these emotions. She wanted to be simple, but her words were always appropriate when she let her heart do the talking. A simple monologue suited the occasion and made me sense her actual joy. The change of her nursing ideals that went from curing to caring was rock solid. She wanted to nurse in a place where caring for patients was at a premium and she found it in the hospice. Her nursing principles easily transformed from saving lives to comforting those without hope of a cure. She wanted to demonstrate to patients that there was meaning in their suffering.

Melanie—the nurse who earned her place by experience

Melanie was my very first research interview. I was on edge, did not trust my interviewing skills. Yet as a nurse I should be used to talking with people. However what I did with patients was not formally interviewing them, it was nurse-patient communication. Is there a difference, I ask? There certainly is. Melanie was not sick, and my role was not that of a clinician, I was a researcher. After a cup of coffee and in spite of my concern about the fancy digital recorder, we managed well.

Melanie told me that she had lived most of her life in South Africa, only recently migrating to Australia with her husband and children. She was an experienced palliative care nurse but recalled how it was not always like that. During her training Melanie was uncomfortable with cardiopulmonary resuscitation and never had the opportunity to apply the procedure to a patient who had a cardiac arrest. Her reason for the discomfort was fed by the belief that you must be successful in resuscitating all patients. After qualifying as a registered nurse Melanie travelled overseas for a holiday.

While in Britain as a private nurse she saw a film about an English hospice. Melanie was fascinated by the 'holistic' patient care, she had not heard of it before, a really 'hands on' nursing care, no drama of intensive active treatment. Patients were allowed to die when their time came.

> *The film showed the importance of the role of the family. I thought this is something that I have felt for so long and felt quite frustrated on the wards during my training when we were in a rush. I often felt that you never had time to be with the family, did not have time to talk to the patient. Wow, this is the type of nursing [hospice] that I would really enjoy it was an eye opener for me. A whole new world.*

She convinced herself that this is what she always wanted to do forgetting her fear of people dying during resuscitation procedures or any other time. However for Melanie, hospice offered more opportunity to spend time with patients, do all the special caring things she missed out on in her general training. So end of life nursing was to be her choice. Without realising it she took on much more than she could cope with as a novice registered nurse. She lacked the understanding for only working without allowing time for play that is so important in the life of palliative care nurses. One must leave death and dying in the hospice. Her obvious inexperience with this caused stress and an early 'burnout'. The nursing director noticed this and suggested she take time out. Melanie loved the work but being young and inexperienced she thought she could do it all. Going to funerals of all the deceased patients, nursing them to the end and supporting grieving relatives took their toll as she recalled:

> *I had not learnt how to put up protective barriers then, and seeing it from a purely cultural point also; the white patients would wait until I was on duty. They did not feel comfortable sharing with the African staff. I reached a point where I had nothing more to give. I felt I did not want to hear another sad story, I did not want to hear another problem.*

An overseas trip again came to the rescue during which Melanie worked in private homes in England for close to three years. She slowly healed and met Michael soon after returning home. They eventually married and two boys were born in quick succession. While the boys were pre-schoolers Melanie worked part time in the local nursing home. In a year or two Michael a Primary School Teacher was offered a post in Abu Dhabi and the family took off for a part of the world they did not know much about. Soon after settling in, Melanie joined the staff of a 'medical diagnostic hospital' as public health care facilities were known in Abu Dhabi. Not long after starting work in the hospital the pastor from the local Christian church asked Melanie for advice concerning a dying woman who was in the Intensive Care Unit (ICU). The Pastor heard that Melanie had past experience in hospice work. The patient she was asked to see was terminally ill but was not allowed to die, the only thing she begged for continuously. Local legislation prescribed treatment for all patients no matter how life threatening their illness was. Roma the European ICU patient in question was resuscitated several times even though she suffered a terminal illness. Melanie accepted the challenge and hoped she could face the dying woman after a long spell away from palliative care.

> *I went to see this poor woman. She had been resuscitated three times already and kept saying she wanted to die. This brought everything back to me . . . everything about hospice.*

Melanie suddenly remembered what gave her the most satisfaction in nursing and what she really wanted to do. She easily sorted out Roma's comfort care by approaching the nurses and doctors in the ICU and eventually the poor woman was allowed to die in relative comfort.

Days that followed saw Melanie's delight in work increase so much so that her husband was prompted to comment that he had not seen her this happy for sometime. Experience with the dying Roma helped

Melanie in regaining her confidence with end of life nursing. Melanie was certain that she was sent a 'sign' to tell her she now was ready to return to her real vocation. The peace and joy she felt at her decision, and Michael noticing the change in her, was comforting.

On the family's return to South Africa she applied for a hospice position remaining there until migrating to Australia. Melanie had no problem getting a position in hospice work soon after her arrival in Australia, and some years later has job satisfaction in her adopted country.

Jennifer—a late starter

I talk about Jennifer here even though most of her palliative care work was practiced in the community, but at the time of the interview she worked in a formal 'in bed' hospice service.

The story of Jennifer the nurse was quite different from most others I interviewed. She was twenty-seven when starting her nurse training. Until then Jennifer for some years was a receptionist in a suburban health clinic. Her nurse colleagues there suggested she should take on studies that would give her formal nursing qualifications. Eventually she qualified as a registered nurse in a large public hospital. Jennifer did not like it much but persevered and after qualifying she took a job in a small country hospital that suited her better. She remained there until, encouraged by nurse colleagues, reluctantly decided on training as a midwife that returned her to city life. 'That was not a happy time either', said Jennifer as she remembered.

> *I hated it and wanted to leave half way through. I was persuaded to at least get a certificate for my troubles. From there I went into district nursing and that was different. I loved it.*

She was the happiest when entering a home that was troubled and leaving it peaceful. She loved the relaxed ambience of patient choices so evident in most home situations.

Our discussion energized Jennifer. Talking of community nursing brought out her best memories. Each turn in the conversation reminded her of why she preferred the less structured patient contact. I identified with a great deal in her practice, even as I was a bedside hospice nurse. My approach to care was also directed by 'patient choices'—ones Jennifer alluded to. As such it could very well be that Jennifer's life experience is the directing force behind her patient care:

> *It gave me a lot of satisfaction [community nursing]. I liked it. You work alone and are responsible for yourself. I gained assessment skills I might never have learnt otherwise.*

I was about to ask Jennifer how she got into palliative care but before I had a chance she went on to tell me how it was for her:

> *What used to happen was that a number of nurses did not want to look after people who were dying at home. It was too hard or very distressing or whatever reason they gave, so I used to take on dying patients and looked after X number of people who wanted to die at home at any one time. I liked that because in my heart I felt that independence is important for dying people. The thing that struck me most about working in the home was the reluctance of family members to take on a caring role initially. They were unsure of their ability to cope, and almost convince the visiting nurse that they could not do it. Yet if you go gently and introduce them slowly to the situation, staying in the background as a support person there generally is a good outcome. As time goes by the family takes over and the nurse becomes a valued friend. Families do like their independence and control to the end, and being involved with the death helps them greatly with their grief management.*

Jennifer's love for community nursing kept her there for some years during which time she formed her ideals about caring for terminally ill people that may have started as far back as her training days:

> *When I think back I did not like people dying in a hospital in my training days, because they always shut people into single rooms. It did not suit me the way they handled people who were dying. When I think about it even back then, in the 70s, we did not give all the comfort they needed, we did not give people the relief they needed. In 30 years though we have come a long way in symptom management.*

Eventually Jennifer decided to transfer to an in house hospice that she developed a liking for. It was attached to one of the universities that had a professorial chair of palliative care assuring a strong focus on care for patients with life limiting illnesses. That is where she was at the time of this interview.

Talking of death and dying developed without fuss. Death is peaceful most of the time if it is managed well. Nurses can do much to smooth the passage of dying for their patients. Jennifer had a healthy attitude to the inevitability of death:

> *I guess, I may have always thought that dying is an important phase as important as any other phase in life, I still feel that way. Terminally ill people and families often don't accept that death is inevitable. I am quietly critical when I'm dealing with them and see that they know what the score is yet don't believe death will ever happen to them. In the back of my mind I ask, why don't these people understand that death is always in everybody's future?*

Jennifer spoke of her comfort with death and dying at the bedside. I asked her how that was possible for her time and time again? 'I am not unhappy with the end', she says:

> *There cannot be a miraculous resurrection. But what you can do is make whatever the time limit is as good as you can. That is important because the big fear people have is how dying could be a disaster, a painful suffering, could be horrible and it does not have to be like that.*

Trust between nurse and patient in palliative care is almost obligatory. The nurse who is comfortable with managing death issues knows how to build trust. Each individual nurse adopts a different skill while becoming an advocate for her sick charges. Jennifer was eloquent about this:

> *Trust is at the base of the palliative relationship. Trusting is when the patient says 'I hand my life to you trusting you to do the best with what I give you, my power'. Remember I said at the beginning that when you go out to people's homes they have got all the power and eventually there is an exchange of that. I then see the palliative relationship evolve and it is a trusting one. The problem often is when patient referral to our care is as late as a couple of days before death and you have to try and establish trust.*

This is when the expertise of the palliative care nurse comes to the fore. Jennifer would have preferred a longer period with her patients but so often these days patients come into an institutional setting to die at a much later stage in their illness. Families try and cope at home as long as humanly possible. Unfortunately there are times when death like birth cannot be managed in a home environment.

Diana—a nurse for all seasons

Diana is one of those people whom I would trust with my life. I worked with her for some years. She is a dear friend, we spend time walking the hills once a week and share the pleasure of symphony concerts to which we subscribe religiously. Getting away from death and dying keeps us mentally healthy. Diana loves football and she is a demon as a spectator, a loyal demon, no matter whether her team wins or loses. It is interesting sitting comfortably in my lounge room with this good friend yet I find some discomfort creeping in as we settled down to start the interview. This sounds strange, I should not have felt uneasy.

Diana was destined to be a nurse. Her mother was the role model even as her father hoped for a university education for his only daughter. Her mother Joan, a retired nurse, was pleased with Diana's choice and encouraged her as much as she could.

Training was partly completed in the country where Diana lived and partly in one of the large training hospitals in the city. She looked upon the days of living in the nurses' home as happy years where making lifelong friendships was the order of the day. Midwifery came as an expected postgraduate qualification. Most nurses from the country automatically did this because obstetrics was mandatory for a nursing position in country hospitals.

Diana and Peter met during this second course that Peter's sister also took. Diana and Peter married after the end of the midwifery course. Peter's job took him around Australia and after giving birth to four children, the family finally returned to Diana's place of birth in a small country town. The first child was in a boarding school in the city, the younger three attended local schools. Diana took up a post of senior nurse in the local aged care facility. When all of the children reached secondary school age the family moved to the city because finding funds for four boarding school fees was rather difficult.

Diana had to find a new job. At the time she had two opportunities to chose from, one being the hospice the other a rehabilitation unit. Eventually she opted for the hospice:

> *I was taken by the hospice . . . when I walked in that door . . . such a lovely place I loved the long corridor and every one had smiles. I had such a peaceful feeling. I cannot remember what made me decide. I think it was that feeling. Everybody smiled and made me welcome after all these years having been in the bush so long. I thought I would give it a try. It was an important time in the history of palliative care.*

For Diana getting into a new team, learning new things was an amazing discovery. She spoke of how she appreciated nurses in the hospice, how she got to love them. She treasured learning new skills, recalling how colleagues taught her so much. The hospice movement started to come into its own at the time Diana joined its staff in the late 1980s. The hospice appointed a new medical director who was trained as a Palliative Care Physician. He brought new ideas that lifted the level of care and offered new insights into end of life medicine and nursing. Diana could not believe her luck to be there at that groundbreaking time:

> *I was in on the ground floor, new ways of approaching care. Then there was the privilege of doing primary nursing where you are able to have continuity of quality care.*

As Diana mentioned, the unit manager introduced the 'primary nursing' model where the admitting nurse was responsible for the patient's continuing management issues. The Hospice staff welcomed and embraced this care model. Diana explained why:

> *Because through continuity is when you really appreciate doing the most basic things for people, things that are not really basic, things that make them comfortable as human beings and give you the opportunity to get close to them. By continuing the care of the same patient, opportunities arise to learn more about that person. You get to know their smallest wishes by observation without having to ask first. You can then have a peaceful flow*

of work; discuss something when the right moment crops up. And you get to know the kind of feelings that go on between the families . . . pick up on the details quite naturally. You can get on to the facts.

Hospice work suited Diana's nursing philosophy. There was not much she would not do for her patients. She was caring, reliable, understanding and was a great 'team' person .Her colleagues liked working with her. The newly built hospice was opened soon after Diana joined the unit, presenting an opportunity for a new, senior, role. She was encouraged to apply. An essentially shy person she declined initially but gave in at the end. She was promoted to second in charge of the unit and ran it as smoothly as clockwork. Diana never talked about her new role. Her first love never changed, she preferred patient contact at the bedside, the hands on patient care. She was ready to help any nurse, patient or relative, and always went off duty late. She loved the work and recalled the medical director's philosophy of patients at the end of their life: 'Michael spoke of enormous spiritual growth in a dying patient when there is true nurturing'. Diana was a 'true nurturer'—patients, relatives and colleagues would readily testify to that.

Then came the change

As much as Diana loved her hospice nursing she missed Peter who had been working on the Australian Aboriginal lands for some time and asked her to join him. It was a difficult decision. She felt as if she was being torn two ways. Peter, also a nurse, had spent the previous four years away from home and the marriage needed to be rekindled in some way. There was no question of whose lifestyle had to change. Diana bade farewell to the hospice and to colleagues who tearfully waved goodbye. I asked her if she had found opportunities to use her palliative care skills on the lands?

There was a brief pause. I think Diana needed to take herself back to the 'lands' [Australian Aboriginal traditional home lands]. While the country there is harsh and unforgiving the people on the other hand got to know and love her in a special way. Diana spent four years there and returned to the hospice about the time of this interview. A piece of her heart remained with the sick Aboriginal women as her answer to my question reflected:

> *Use my palliative care skills? A lot of my patients were very sick. In a sense you could say a lot of them were palliative care. A lot of them had bronchiectasis [lung disease] as children. In their fifties and sixties they were living on powerful antibiotics. I had three old ladies who came for postural drainage regularly [to clear their lungs] and I found it was the biggest privilege to spend emotional time with them. I do their drainage and they honour me by singing their chant in that raucous voice in their rhythmic way.*

Diana went on softly talking about that chant in the clinic room. I joined in the feeling as we envisaged channelling into the aboriginal spirituality:

> *Yes, and when I left one of my favourites, such a little fighter, she had no lung capacity, none whatsoever, yet made me a beanie [woollen cap], it was so special. Having worked in palliative care before I was able to develop that very close relationship maybe, I don't know maybe I even did have that before then.*

Returning to the hospice after four years of providing continuous and often twenty-four hour 'on call' care for the Aboriginal community, Diana settled back once more into the relatively organised life of the hospice nurse, doing permanent night work. She was glad to be a nurse at the bedside again and the night work assured a level of autonomy. Diana at this stage of her life wanted nothing more than to do what she liked best, comforting patients. Night work presented an ideal environment for this because night-time brings extra fears that daytime often hides:

> *I think, I am very fortunate in doing night duty and by and large I have a great team to work with. At night I can devote better quality time to the patients because there is less pressure of organisational politics to cope with, you can be a good nurse.*

These five nurses showed a preference for institutional palliative care. They spent many years working in hospice settings looking after patients who could not be managed in the home. The quality of their nursing care was the same as that of palliative carers everywhere, only the venue was in an institutional setting.

Interestingly though more than half of the nurses I interviewed were community palliative carers. I wondered if the reason for this is the more autonomous thinking of these nurses who found it easier to be independent. The formative nursing years of this group like those in the institutional setting was spent in various areas of hospital work, and the transfer to palliative care followed on the nurses' gaining clinical expertise in their later years.

Palliative Care in the Community: an affirming experience of dying in the home—four voices

Uncertainty created by a life threatening illness is the same whether in hospital or in the sick person's home, where nurses are not the primary carers. The role of the nurse in the home situation is that of an invited guest and adviser. Entering someone else's private domain the nurse is no longer in charge. Even when in an invited professional capacity she still has to conform to the household conventions where the daily routine differs from that of a hospital. My interviewees working in the home, developed a good relationship with the family, and became a part of their joy and sorrow at a vulnerable time. Increased autonomy for both the patient and the nurse afforded by the home environment was another benefit because as Jennifer said:

> *The nurse could delegate power to the patient. It is they who direct the care. The visiting nurse is there to encourage and support the patient's independence. It does not always work out but it can be managed successfully more often than not resulting in the patient being in control. You as the nurse just contribute what you know or what you have to give, but really it is their life and they should be in control and do what they want or can.*

In the community, nurses are also the automatic link to medical help facilitating a more intimate care management. How it all works is best told by those who actually do the work.

Sue

The following could easily be a summary of most nurses who work in patients' homes. Sue like others in district nursing developed a liking for community nursing early in her career. She did not particularly like hospital work, Intensive Care, Accident and Emergency were too 'high powered' for her. She just wanted to be at the bedside, provide basic nursing care, talk to patients and treat them with dignity:

> *And that is why I liked district nursing and that is how it was probably for the first fifteen years of my working life, and my interest in palliative care started in community nursing.*

Sue remembered how caring for people at the end of life in their homes made nursing not only a working relationship but also a daily joy such as being with the grieving family after the patients' death, as in Bob's case:

> *When he died the family rang me, and when I visited they asked me if I wanted a private moment with him. This happens often because the family feels we also need to say farewell, they embrace us [nurses] as a part of the family. I sat with Bob for 10 minutes and when I came out there were lots of hugs, chitchat of happy memories. Then they asked me to help write the death notices, asked me to help with the wording. This was very special, and explains why I take something with me every time I look after someone who died. One family did not quite understand what I meant by that, thinking I wanted to cut a lock of their dad's hair. I told them this taking something is on a spiritual level.*

I suddenly remembered the death of my husband at home. While Steven managed well, he always welcomed the visit of the hospice nurse who became a close friend to both of us. Steven did not make friends easily especially with nurses, yet he welcomed Erin at every visit spending time discussing more than his cancer.

Sue put a high value on being trusted by the family that according to her was built on:

> *Unconditional acceptance from the time I walk through the front door for the first time. They [the family] are aware that I am there to help. I love that ease of connectivity with people whom I have not met before and will never see again. I provide basic care essentially, but do it with a strong emotional component.*

Eve

Eve whose early palliative care was practiced in the community also said that way back when she did not have much experience, she was adamant that terminally ill people should die at home in control of their lives right to the end with nursing support. Later though she found that it was not practicable in all cases. But while she did home care Eve was always conscious of people's boundless ability and energy to manage death outside institutional care. She readily picked this up at the time with her youthful sensitivity:

> *Families have such strength, and the way they manage to deal with looking after somebody till the end, until they [patients] become unconscious, is amazing. That is what I love about family members, staying up all night no medical or nursing background and somehow they find the strength and knowledge to do it. I want to stay working with people, I like going into a room with a patient, doing simple things. Checking the bed for comfort, or wetting a dry mouth. I always thought that nursing is being with people, looking after people, and helping them to feel better about themselves. I realized this very early as a student nurse.*

Chris

Practicing primarily in the community before commencing a full time PhD program Chris was a strong advocate for patients dying at home. He saw himself in the role of a guest there and believed that he was obliged to respect that place and all that it meant to those living there [patients' home]. Chris strongly argued for how and where patients should die, the 'how' component signalling his low tolerance for the possible over use of medicalised symptom management. He maintained that patients at end of their lives benefit more from being in a familiar environment than from excessive drug management.

Whilst I accepted this as partly valid, coming from a hospice environment I made a case for how most patients on admission to the unit without some drug supported symptom management would die in agony, but with appropriate symptom management they often rallied. Frequent experience with short-term hospice inpatients meant that I found that those precious few days after good symptom management provided the dying person with strength and capacity to organize matters such as writing a will, saying goodbye to family and friends, visiting home or discussing funeral arrangements.

Liz

The story of Liz, the community nurse in the city is a special one. I met her initially when she cared for one of my hospice patients at home. She made a point of visiting him before discharge to make his acquaintance and speak with me about any treatment issues. Liz was the senior Clinical Nurse Consultant in Palliative Care with the local District Nursing Services. I was always comfortable when she took over the care of one of my patients.

Her passage into palliative care was directed by her young brother's death number of years earlier when she was in her mid nursing career. Married with a young baby at the time Liz was elected by her family to deal with the hospital and the doctors treating Luke [her brother]. He had many problems as Liz recalled:

> I was in and out of the hospital and I met obstacles at every step put there by the nurses looking after him. They saw it as their duty to keep all information about the diagnosis from Luke and me.

Her brother's untimely death was heart breaking because of the specialist physician's determination to treat him until the day he died. Liz spoke of how from then on she devoted her professional life to nursing people who were coming to the end of theirs. She remembered many amazing cases that involved families who were dedicated, uncomplaining, and highly effective home nurses. According to Liz she felt rather insignificant in the face of all what family members had to cope with. Liz sang praises of the people in her care, the patients and the families, barely mentioning what she did and how she coped. I could not help but admire this selfless approach:

> *I feel that I am just a little tiny part that gets them [the family] through the day. Really they are an inspiration, they are the ones that do all the work. The families, we expect them to be nurses, doctors, social workers. In the home they administer morphine, and they never make a mistake. I've never seen any one get it wrong. They are so 'spot on'.*

Quietly I reminded her that none of the home care would be possible without professional support. Without her teaching the family they could have fear, be uncertain and even panic at times.

We talked about palliative care in general, a specialty that needs more devotion than any other branch of nursing. We both agreed that the nurse in Palliative Care has to get it right the first time because we only die once. Give the wrong advice, the wrong support and the damage will be irreparable for the surviving family members. Liz looked at me and said with warmth and enthusiasm:

> *It is not like diabetes, where the patient can have a second admission to hospital and you can right the wrong. In palliative care this is it, there is only one opportunity and we have to get it right.*

I felt at ease in Liz's presence and did more than just listen to her story. I unconsciously shared in her journey as I was reminded of episodes in my nursing days that were special. Talking with her recalled feelings I had at the bedside of my dying patients. Being with Liz became a meeting of like-minded souls as we drifted away from the interview's main purpose. During this meeting I frequently had to remind myself that this is not a social call for coffee and catch up but a serious research data collecting mission. Still I am not apologising for the way I felt about this interview. Liz has this effect on patients, families and colleagues alike. Her developed into the embodiment of palliative nursing continues to amaze me. Wanting her company is a proof of my continued devotion to patient care.

Rural Community Palliative Care—three voices

My next trip was to a rural hospice service where I interviewed outreach nurses who dealt with palliative care management of terminally ill patients in outlying farming properties as well as in the township where they were situated. In country areas nurses had to cope with intricacies of long distance travel for patient visits. This out reach work was more demanding than that in the town because of nurses on occasions experienced difficulties with gaining access to remote farms. Barbara testified to such an incident: '*I like a challenge. I don't think I ever not got through a door but I've been thrown out once*' is how she described the dangers in out of the way country places.

For the country nurse living and working in a close-knit community adds problems of privacy to an already taxing workload. This often is in the shape of accidental meetings with client connections from the past, while shopping as Alex remembers:

> *Some days you just can't be bothered. When it is your day off you need that time out. I don't want to sit there and talk with them about the family. I don't want to be nasty. But I need time out, you need boundaries otherwise you cannot continue the work.*

On the other hand rural communities, because they are so close-knit, look upon the hospice service as their very own. Community support for the hospice workers was readily available in this town, I met a group of hospice volunteers during their monthly meeting over freshly baked scones and cakes. Their role varied from fund raising to sitting with dying patients. Alex commented on this:

> *Yes, it is different here, especially in this community. This organization [the hospice service] has had a really good name for many years. The service given to patients is very humbling and you feel very privileged when you say you work here.*

I felt so comfortable in this environment where the welcome for my visit was exceptional. The stories the nurses told me certainly demonstrated their attitude to people and their care of the patients. It was not always easy with some families' mistrust of strangers the first time, no matter how helpful the nurses were.

Barbara

Barbara's visit to a farming property describes well what I mean. She spoke of a day when she visited a farm where she was admitted inside the house, the male patient however was an unhappy disgruntled customer rejecting the openhearted nurse initially. The family welcomed her though, freely accepting her offer of help:

> *He was a very, very difficult man. Blood transfusions kept him alive and he was angry. Previously two of our nurses came back in tears after visiting him in the hospital, I knew it wouldn't be easy. When I got there I talked about our service and how we could help him and his wife. During the time I was there, an hour and fifteen minutes, and I had my hands tightly clutched under the table all that time because he was baiting me. I knew he was baiting me. It was lunchtime and I was ready to leave. As a parting gesture he said 'Barbara, I was trying and trying to get you to raise your voice several times, I tried to put you on a spot and you did not catch on. You answered my questions appropriately you never raised your voice and thank you for that'. I did then leave to tee up another lot of blood for him. He died that weekend. I saw him several times and built up a lovely rapport with his family. His wife was magic, she still comes to the memorial service that is a regular event for patients who died under our care, six years down the track.*

The image of this visit calls to mind a situation that often happens when the patient is not comfortable. Yes, in my own hospice practice I found that the so-called difficult patient was predominantly the one in pain, frightened, sad or angry at the disease that is slowly killing him This is when acceptance, tolerance and not being judgmental pay dividends.

Another day Barbara was denied admission to another farm. Her discomfort and possible danger did not stop her trying to get to see the Patient. She eventually was allowed in. Why did she persist? I asked. In her inimitable style that she calls 'ordinariness' reminded me that hospice nurses never give up and accept what comes with good grace. We laughed at this because it was so true. We all did this. Barbara then went on with the story:

> *There were so many down and out people I cared for. They probably brought me as much pleasure as the people who had everything. This takes me back to another time where I was again told that I would not get through the front door. The patient was a middle-aged man living with his mother who was also dying. She had been referred to our service several years before but refused the offer of help.*

Since this was a case of helping her son who was suffering head and neck cancer, the old lady let Barbara in and chatted pleasantly while agreeing to further visits. It was just as well because the mother was found dead during one of the regular calls on her son. From then on Tom was left to live on his own with an old dog as his sole companion. He had a painful neck wound needing daily dressing changes that was usually done by the district nurse. One day this nurse phoned Barbara in an agitated state. She was upset because the dog kept removing the dressing and licking Tom's wounds 'The dog has to go,' said she. Barbara recalled that this happened only two days before Tom died, her reply to the nurse was: 'Let him be we will look in on him. We kept him at home with the dog, as long as need be.'

Alex

Alex contributed a favourite story of the first visit to a farm where she found the family sitting on the patient's bed and feeding the semi-conscious man with ice cream. That was when Alex for the first became aware of the difference between this and hospital work. She sat down on the bed while changing the syringe driver and chatted with the family. There was laughter and closeness without the routine of a hospital, where the nurse could not sit on the bed and the dying man would definitely not be offered food of any kind.

This opened an avalanche of stories from Sonia. She spoke of others but another one stood out as truly remarkable. She recalled her involvement with a middle-aged couple living on their farm, happy in a second marriage until Tim was diagnosed with a brain tumour. Alex remembered how the patient/nurse relationship evolved from the day of her first visit. Alex first met the couple in the hospital after Tim's operation. Eventually he was sent home with the knowledge that he might not live longer than two months. As it often happens

Tim became a long-term involvement for all three of the nurses, much longer than the promised two months. Alex being the first visitor developed a close relationship with the couple leading to an ongoing friendship with the widow even after Tim died. This is not always advisable but Alex managed this relationship well by pulling out when Mary the widow settled down to a single life.

Mara

Mara, the senior member of this rural palliative care service was responsible for setting up the unit. Her main role is grief management, but she is also still involved with clinical patient care. She assured me that transferring her practice in midlife from intensive care to hospice work was not only timely but also rewarding. She recalled that while working in an Intensive Care Unit (ICU) discovered how often it was the being with a patient that made the difference not the regular recorded half hourly observations. I use Mara's words to give this the credit it deserves. It would be difficult to put it better:

> *I think ICU brings you to a state of nursing where you think beyond the square, and you look at the responsibility you take and the actions you do, in other words you think deeper by looking beyond that. You go in there, you learn about a huge number of machines yet when it comes to the crunch you look at the patient first. The machines are only tools it is the patient who matters. It is powerful stuff, looking behind the 'machines' was an invaluable lesson.*

In the 1980s Mara was persuaded to take on the new specialty of palliative care without any educational support. Since palliative care was in its infancy education was not available initially. Mara however managed to set up a palliative care support service in her rural area that she went on managing to the time and beyond our interview.

Mara's enthusiasm for palliative care took me back to the exciting times of the 80s when palliative care was comparatively new in Australia. She described how setting up the unit twenty years earlier was an exciting task. This then developed into the focus of her working life. But 'Mara the hands on nurse' was never too far from clinical work when called to do so.

Mara spoke openly of personal grief issues as well such as the death of her own mother that impacted on her role with grieving relatives giving her a better understanding for family bereavement. I rather enjoyed her no holds barred description of being in this rural community where things are open and honest:

> *You cut the crap. You develop relationships with people where you don't have to do the social dances. It is actually about mutual respect it is about the fact that once you establish communication people will talk about things very close to their hearts that makes dying much less difficult to bear.*

Yet we are so often prevented from being humanly present with patient, I thought, because of the 'frills' that we are required to attach to our daily practice. I recall the times I had to stop and complete a new chart dreamt up by a bureaucratic nurse to prove in writing that I actually did the caring I was expected to do. The writing always held me up and the only way I could manage it was by doing unpaid overtime. As far as I was concerned the dying patient was so much more important

So different yet so alike

These extracts from interview transcripts are special segments of the whole. I found them significant because they include outstanding examples of and strong emphasis on the ideals of palliative care practice. At every step there is empathy, care and love in a strong competent practitioner who is a committed patient advocate.

The interviewed nurses were from varied backgrounds. Beside bedside nursing and working in community hospice care there were the ones who contributed to palliative care in another role. Jennifer at the time of the interview was the nurse-manager of a purpose built hospice in an Australian seaside township. She not only managed the unit but was responsible for setting up a community service also. She came to this from years of experience in surgical and medical nursing as well as midwifery.

In another diverse role Sue, the competent palliative care nurse with years of service in the community, changed tack. After leaving palliative care she completed a midwifery program. Sue then used her experience in grief management in a different yet similar role to that of hospice work in a maternity hospital. There she counselled parents who lost newborn infants, had spontaneously aborted pregnancies, or faced premature or disabled babies in the neonatal intensive care unit.

Chris was completing a full time PhD program in palliative care where his research was into setting up palliative care support in the community. Scott lectured undergraduate nursing students in palliative care additionally to his clinical managerial role in a hospice unit.

What brought all of them together as co-researchers was their practical knowledge about terminally ill and dying patients' pain and suffering. The result of this was the understanding of how they envisaged their palliative care practice, and how they got there in the first place. Their words resounded with ideals which I also held dear. I came from the same place and practiced the craft they practiced.

Chapter 2
Inner Secrets of Being There at the End of Life of the Other

Why did these nurses change?

The research question seeks the identity of the dynamics that influenced nurses' decision to leave the environment of healing and transfer to people suffering terminal illnesses from which there is no hope of a recovery. It asks why and when qualified general nurses take on palliative care as a career option. The answer talks to who the nurse is, where she comes from and what brought about the change in caring ideals.

My study is directed by evocative auto-ethnography that speaks with stories, which could have more than one interpretation. I want to tell a very good story because I discovered so much in others that had also been a part of me. I could easily talk about my personal passion for palliative care because I know where that comes from, but that is my story. Auto-ethnography is open to and suggests inclusion of 'others' in the study who could contribute to my story. I have reviewed my range of vision, and I have arrived at the point of my horizon where I only see so far and not beyond it. Fusing it with that of other palliative care nurses' perspectives raised my vision to a point beyond and above the past and present, gaining a broader panorama that might even project into the future.

With my eyes wide open I now go on

I re-read the well-worn piece of literature that says 'Hospice nurses are generally acknowledged by other nurses . . . to be special'. I always found this observation a little too robust, and was quick to ask 'why should that be so?' However, most people come across death only a few times in their lives in contrast to nurses in hospice and palliative care. Could this observation justify palliative care nurses being seen as 'special', and be the substance of the 'difference' that many recognized as the significant difference in palliative care nursing? Or would a simple observation like the one by Jill a bedside clinician, clarify this:

> *People who actually don't know anything about palliative care think you are a special person when in actual fact you yourself think you are a bit selfish because you think you are getting more from the patient than you are giving them.*

One formal question at the start

I started each interview with the question of why participants became nurses. To start with my aim with this was to ask why nursing attracted this group of people in the first place. The reasons given ranged widely. The influence of *'mother as role model'* was a popular concept for a number of co-researchers like Diana and Beth. Their mothers were former nurses. Diana's early Christmas presents were dress up nurses' uniforms with play thermometer and stethoscope. Another preferred reason was *'family background'* playing a significant role for example in Sue's choice for nursing. Sue's family had strong community awareness where helping others was of considerable importance. Her story supported her statement. Rosalie wanted *'independence'*. When all hope was gone for a teaching future that would rescue her from parental supervision in country Britain, she went for the next best thing, and that in her opinion was nursing. There were no training schools near where she lived so she had to go to the city to apply for entry. Ellen who also did not make grades to study teaching chose nursing that fulfilled her idea for working with people. However, before commencing her nurse training she worked in a factory that gave her a taste for being with a variety of people. That seemed a good preparation for nursing.

Training for the register was *'change of roles within the health care culture'* for Scott and Jennifer. They both worked in the health industry before formally training for the register as nurses. Scott was a nurse assistant in an aged care facility and Jennifer a receptionist in a large health clinic. They eventually found their niche as registered nurses and had no regrets. All this came at the right time in their life and maturity in age made palliative care a relatively early career choice for both.

Opting for a nursing career after '*experience of close family death*' for Chris came with the death of his grandmother when he was alone with her at the age of sixteen. He decided to be a nurse changing his first choice that was to be teaching. He never diverged from that decision.

Family death came early into Kathy's life when she was only fifteen and her forty-year-old father died with cancer. She spent a lot of time in the hospital sitting at his side and noting the gentle way nurses applied themselves to easing her father's final days. Kathy decided she would train as a nurse as soon as she completes her high school education.

Melanie experienced hospital life as a child patient. When only four years old she suffered third degree burns to a large part of her body requiring long distance travel for a number of years to have specialist treatment. Her nurses and the plastic surgeon left a lasting impression with their compassionate caring. Melanie recalled how the medical and nursing environment at the time provided the *positive medical role model* that influenced her future. She remembered fondly the very last hospital visit, when she was a teenager, one of the nurses asked her help with badly burnt soldiers situated in the next ward. After that there was no doubt in her mind that she would be happiest studying to be a nurse.

Pat, Jennifer, Liz, Barbara, Jill and Mara were *not as specific* about their initial reason for a nursing career. Yet most spoke fondly of training days and family support through some difficult periods. Alex always wanted to be a nurse, not giving a reason why. There were no role models to inspire her, but she was adamant that nursing was what she would want to do. Scott was looking for a career that would be secure with opportunity for promotion with an income that would enable him to provide adequately for his wife and children.

These stories supported my understanding that nursing was not a random choice for these people. It was a determined decision for a profession that offered possibility for diverting within its boundaries of varied specialties.

Interest in holistic patient management

I noticed a palpable emotional characteristic in the group I was working with: distress at the way the care of patients in the areas they were transferring from was strongly directed at physical problems. When on duty in surgical or medical wards it seemed to them that they were ignoring the emotional aspects that affected not only the patient but also the family. This 'medicalised' approach is illustrated by Mara in the Intensive Care Unit (ICU) where she had many such experiences that she has never forgotten. Mara was visibly emotional when telling one of her stories:

> *I was working in ICU at the base hospital on nights and looking after a lady who was basically brain dead but was still actively managed, we were doing full observations half hourly stuff* [routine work] *and it was quite obvious that she was brain dead. I spent a lot of my time talking with distressed family members while going through the motions of regularly checking the pulse blood, pressure and the likes. It was an intense time. The younger family members were very distressed when the respirator was turned off. I had to explain what was going to happen, talk about death that would eventually follow. It was really rather lovely to know that the half hourly observations were not actually making any difference, but being there did. That was powerful stuff f... looking behind the 'machines'. It was an invaluable lesson.*

Mara makes it clear in this example that she could easily have taken the observations and left the bedside to continue her other routine work. Instead she lingered, she used the clinical observations as an opportunity to participate in what became a rather detailed conversation with the family that involved medical, emotional and personal perspectives.

Rosalie, reflected on the time just before leaving ICU for hospice work, and shared her feelings that influenced her transfer:

> *Lots of the patients I felt were not in the right place. They used to call me 'the death queen' because I would be very much inclined to look after people whom I felt were dying, they* [other nurses] *were very worried to look after that* [dying] *lady and I was happy to do it. Whereas a lot of the nurses in that area shied away from death because they saw it as a failure, I never did. And I guess I had worked in intensive care for long enough by*

> *then to recognise that . . . a lot of people in that area used to get a buzz out of patients arresting saying 'have I got him back' being the operative term. I used to find that really troublesome . . . running on your adrenaline . . . it really was not me.*

Nurses like Mara and Rosalie reached a stage in clinical work when there was a wish to be more concerned with the wholeness of body, mind and spirit. This is an often-difficult aim in the busy atmosphere of curing and saving lives at all cost in the world of acute medicine. I recall that in the hospice there was always time to see the patient as a whole person when existential care was on the agenda. This alerted me to the concept of holistic patient management. I could not think of a better way to interpret co-researchers' way of palliative care than seeing it through a holistic lens.

Psychological and emotional needs of dying patients

In giving credit to palliative carers' qualities I am joined by co-researchers in agreeing that as hospice nurses that, besides accountability for our patients' physical comfort, we are responsible for the psychological needs of the dying person in our care.

Much of the work in psychosocial care of the dying patient is in the support for the emotional turmoil taking place in the patient's mind. The existential distress at the time of dying can be a threat to personhood. The sensitive nurse is usually the first one to notice an existential problem and is the one who is able to initiate management. This has been referred to by community nurses in the study especially those responsible for patients' welfare in outlying farming properties. They frequently had to cope with acute distress of patients where they were the first to be confronted with a psychological emergency. While Liz's patient emergency was not purely psychological it had a large element of the existential. David, Liz's patient, was slowly dying in the family home. His wish was to remain there to the end. Jan, his wife, all but gave up the idea in face of the extended family's pressure to force him to transfer to the local hospice.

A tearful Jan greeted Liz one morning and told her how lost she felt, how she did not know what to do. Liz listened to this and decided to stand by Jan, and help her in her quest, no matter what the rest of the family wanted:

> *I thought she [Jan] is young she is motivated she loves him. I said I would help. That very night Jan again got a phone call from the oncologist niece who said, 'You're doing your husband a disservice. He should be in hospital. What are you going to do if he chokes, what are you going to do if this happens?' Jan had a sleepless night and when I got there the next morning I asked: 'How is it going?' She dissolved into tears. We then had a heart to heart talk. I heard about the phone call. The niece also said if Jan gives him morphine she could kill him. I then said: 'This is about you David and the children and not the oncologist niece'. 'David wants to stay at home', added Jan. 'Well what makes you think we cannot do it?' I asked her. 'I am in your team. David is the head of our team: he is the most important person here; you tell him, and just tell the others to stay away. This has nothing to do with them.' Jan then asked: 'Can I do it?' I answered: 'Yes, you are his wife, and the children will also help.'*

This is a situation frequently seen in community palliative care. Extended families do interfere; they may do it with the best of intentions. To avoid family clashes the nurse at times is called to mediate. It takes a nurse with insight and strength to help carry out the last wish of a dying patient. Logistics are often difficult. Terminal care in the home presents many obstacles but they can be overcome most of the time. It is the trust between the nurse and the family that provides the carers with confidence to carry on. Liz believed in leaving the dying patient with control and a lot of dignity.

Two principles: 'acknowledging death' and 'presence'

Acknowledging death and the question of personal mortality

My understanding of the difference that exists between palliative care and general nursing rests predominantly with two basic principles. These differences are, firstly, the acceptance of the concept of death and dying, and secondly, a constant holistic nursing presence with the dying patient. Without these, it seems to me, palliative care would lose its reason for being.

Not many people will face death and dying with a quiet acceptance and understanding, yet it is well known that, like birth, death is an outcome of being alive. This is a profound statement but one that those who intend to manage terminally ill patients need to acknowledge. Working with the culture of serious illness and death requires the presence of a nurse or physician who is emotionally strong enough to develop a philosophical style that enables coping with the daily exposure to suffering – often a number of times each day. It is a tough assignment, but when mastered it pays dividends.

Emotional involvement with serious illness of others calls for a special caring devotion and understanding. Dr Weisman in a lecture to medical students, before allowing them to have contact with patients who were dying, reminded them not to feel guilty that patients are dying 'and you are living. Your time will also come'.[1] In a way Dr Weisman's observation in a single sentence dealt both with death of the patient and the clinicians' attitude to personal mortality.

Nurses in palliative care are reminded of death and dying on a daily basis. That is why acceptance of personal mortality is one of the main and unique nursing attributes of the palliative care nurse without which end of life caring would lose its distinctive character. It would be virtually impossible to nurse people with a life limiting illness when uneasy about demise of the self.

Human existence is limited—palliative care nurses know

Palliative care nurses openly talk of the end of life and admit when they have a problem in meeting it directly. Alex did so when I asked how she deals with death in her professional life:

> *Sometimes there is this bit of fear there. Because we are shown that you could be quite ok one week and the next week your life can actually be turned upside down. That is actually what is so good about our job. Every day we are shown how precious our life is. At the back of my mind I have this slight fear that it could happen to my partner or me one day. You sort of don't want to think about it, but is in the back of your mind.*

Coming from Alex this could be attributed to her relative youth, being in her late twenties. Nurses in the older age group were not troubled in this regard. Or at least they managed any individual difficulties easier.

---

1. AD Weisman, 'The Psychiatrist and the Inexorable', in *New Meanings of Death*, edited by H Feifel (New York: McGraw-Hill, 1977), 110.

They faced personal mortality with a more accepting philosophy like Barbara who spoke of her upbringing as significant for later hospice work:

> *We always had elderly people living with us in a Granny flat down at the back. My grand parents died at home so we were not afraid of dying. We were not told not to go down there because grandma was very ill. We continued on seeing her, she was part of the family. I was not brought up to be afraid of death.*

Jennifer, who came to nursing later than most, spoke freely about mortality. During hospital training she came across nurses who left dying patients in agony. She had little tolerance for that. Discomfort with giving adequate pain relief often indicated a lack of drug administration skills by the nurse. A reluctance to give pain relief is at times caused by fear of hurting the patient; it indicates a fear of mortality. Jennifer maintains that she:

> *always thought that dying is an important phase as important as any other in the lifecycle and I still feel the truth of that. I don't understand why people don't accept that death is always in everybody's future. It is like forgetting that when there is life there is also death.*

Jennifer also recalled when only twelve years old her favourite uncle suddenly died. Jennifer thinks this could have influenced her ease with death and dying because the uncle was like a sibling for her:

> *I still remember I think I was about twelve. I had an old uncle who died; he would have been called retarded. These days he would have been sent to a remedial school but not then. He lived with our family. And he was a good friend to me just like a child. And he died when I was about twelve and it was very distressing for my mother because she looked after him for many years. It was like one of her children dying. So that was important for me to comfort her, I just recall comforting her, and it still stands out after all these years*

Beth's example of the loving way her family dealt with the ritual of laying out the body of their dead father was a testimony to acceptance of mortality, not only by her but also by the rest of her family. This came as a surprise for her because she expected to cope alone, but not so this time:

> *We were all there, all eight of us [siblings] and our mother. It was wonderful because I learnt so much about my brothers and sisters. They were so keen to be a part of that process. And being the nurse I thought I could get one person to help me to lay our father out, just the two us, but the others did not leave the room, they sort of all staid. One of them getting the shaving cream, the other cleaning hair out of the comb and two of us were washing him [father] while someone trimmed his moustache. It was such a beautiful experience about a family loving each other, and being comfortable with death.*

Eve had unusually conflicting attitudes to death. At first I got the impression she had the excitement of the young in a challenging role that she admitted to without me questioning her. Later in the interview she spoke of finding other attractions about being with lonely terminally ill patients and sitting with them: '*When I listened to the soft voices I found it quite rewarding. Other thing that I got from it personally was a kind of a relationship. People wanted me back to look after them and people really liked who I was.*' This was not the usual admission by interviewees about their reason for being with dying patients, and the word 'challenge' came into the discussion. I was confused about this unusual woman who for sometime in her career did not really know where she was going. That could have easily accounted for her early 'burn out'. Yet Eve was not averse to patients dying right from the start of her training. In fact for a while I almost believed that she had a strange fascination for it:

> *I did have that intense time with cancer patients. I guess I saw cancer patients everywhere in the hospital, medical wards, everywhere I went as a student. I guess that intrigued me and kind of challenged me. I felt my work, as a nurse was not just doing the basic stuff, there was more to it. As I got more confident as a student nurse I would actually do more. I give cancer patients a wash and stay there longer because as I was washing them I was asking them questions.*

Cindy a hospice clinician referred to death and dying with respect to family bereavement at first but became passionate when referring to death in the hospice. Cindy had a somewhat similar attitude to that of Eve towards working with dying patients, though her response to being appreciated had a less forceful feel to it. She was gently appreciative:

> *There is incredible job satisfaction in this type of nursing because people are grateful for what you do. There are not too many jobs where people keep on thanking you. In palliative care you get to know the patients at a special time of their life and is a privilege to be a part of their dying. And really you are privy to one of the most extra ordinary experiences of life. And I respect and feel very privileged to be playing a part.*

Chris, while not directly addressing death, expanded eloquently on the end of life of his grandmother and how it impacted on his future career options. He spoke of how he initially wanted to be a teacher but changed his mind:

> *A pivotal event for me that has contributed to that decision and everything that followed was that when I was 15 I was alone with my grandmother who had a cardiac arrest and died and, you know, when you are 15 years old and you are an angst ridden youth, you have all those questions about identity and meaning . . . I was very influenced by this experience. And the overwhelming legacy of witnessing my grandmother's death was the realization that some people get time between knowing that they are going to die and dying – that she did not.*

Chris said that the death of his Grandmother influenced him to learn how to support people who have time to think about their death. In depth study of palliative care was his way of carrying out his promise.

No matter of the difference in their personalities, ages or gender roles nurses in the interviews faced death of their patients with understanding because they accepted that death was a natural event.

Presence—a significant factor

Terminally ill patients are highly sensitive to the behaviour of others, and to being excluded. In the hospice when attending to a patient who is called a 'double', indicating difficulties with mobility issues, a supporting nurse is required. I assumed that we would both include the patient in any conversation and not discuss personal matters while we worked, even if the patient appeared non-responsive. In my experience a dying person senses when the nurse is not fully present. It is a fact that even unconscious patients may hear as they are being spoken about. Rosalie in her interview described a young woman she nursed in Intensive Care who was in an induced coma for some weeks following major abdominal surgery. Rosalie never missed talking to her about the weather, what happened out in the world and even shared her own family stories with the patient who was to all intents and purposes unconscious. One day the young woman was well enough to be brought out of the coma and one of the first things she said to Rosalie when again fully conscious: "Thank you for talking to me when I could not answer and also for giving me extra back rubs that I so enjoyed." Day after day the young woman came up with stories she heard while in an unconscious state, a rare and unusual reaction from a patient. The more I thought about this the more I wanted to share my idea of nursing presence.

Palliative care nurses excel in observational skills that among others are often arrived at through active 'true personal presence' with the patient. The strength of presence is like a precious jewel that can light up a slowly dwindling life. It is an element that connects the nurses' heart and head, and 're-instils caring'.[2] This caring involves knowledge that links to a presence in the moment of connecting. This is when you become aware of yourself, which is the key to being present in the environment. Authier adds that 'being present with others is truly the gift of caring'.[3] In complete presence one is not only physically there, but by letting go of personal concerns one can easily concentrate on the here and now.[4] This 'holistic therapeutic intervention [creates

---

2. P Authier, 'Being Present—The Choice that Re-instills Caring', *Nursing Administration Quarterly*, 28/4 (2004): 276-279.
3. Authier, "Being Present", 276.
4. P Benner, & J Wruebel, editors, *The Primacy of Caring* (Menlo Park, California:

a] healing environment'[5] and at the same time frees one of personal anxieties. This does not ask for time spent with but asks to be 'really' there even if only fleetingly. The nurse experiences this togetherness mostly during 'hands on' care of the patient.

I was appreciative of Mara's strength in sharing a special time of 'being with' a young mother as she was dying in her home even though it made her tearful. I offered to stop but Mara insisted on going ahead with the interview. She wanted to tell me about the time at this farming property that for her was a special event.

> *The team was caring for a mother of three young children in her own home. She had a catastrophic bleed and said she should really go into hospital because her husband won't be able to look after her. She was very compassionate a beautiful-beautiful woman. I actually spent round about, on and off, 15 hours with her that particular day . . . the family made a decision not to have her go to hospital. It was a very intensive period for all of us. I managed very well, I sat on her bed, we talked and listened. It was very much a situation of her last few hours with the kids. Let them sit on the bed, do mum's hair, wash her hands. It was rather a beautiful feeling in a way.*

Meaning making—a summary

The way palliative care nurses practice their craft is interwoven with why they chose to be in the speciality. Our narratives show how a combination of my personal experiential input, together with other nurses' storied lives is able to demonstrate our combined rationale behind the preference for palliation ahead of cure.

In the next section I gather a range of co-researcher responses to my over-arching question. I then add my personal perspective, and finally offer some suggestions to those nurses who may follow in our footsteps.

Here I want to remind the reader that I only discuss the research question throughout the body of the research, I do not actually put it in the form of a question as such.

Addison Wesley Publishing Company, 1989),
5. P Zikorus, 'The Importance of a Nurse's Presence', *Holistic Nursing Practice*, 21/4 (2007): 208-210, 209.

Responses my co-researchers gave to my over-arching question

The initial question of why my interviewees took up nursing as a career moved comfortably into discussion about their specialised work in palliative care. The free-flowing nature of our conversations soon focussed on the reasons for nursing in this field, and the dialogue between like-experienced people produced some interesting outcomes. My co-researchers had commonality on several fronts that made evident similar caring characteristics—and some unexpected ones.

Not a vocational metamorphosis

With the majority of the group career transformation was not a vocational metamorphosis, as I believed before listening to them individually. Instead, I discovered that most had significant basic vocational attributes even before contemplating nursing as a career. Pre-disposing situations that emphasised most of the meaning behind early vocational traits were:

- Early life experience with death (Chris and Becci)
- Family upbringing, caring, sharing, open honest relationship within the family unit, community involvement (Sue)
- Spirituality (Cindy)
- Sensitivity to life and love for those who are weaker (Rosalie)
- Humble, gentle and caring parents as role models (Diana)
- A level of religious belief (Cindy, Chris)

Experience in clinical practice

Experience was the most common directing force responsible for the change in caring ideals. The general term 'experience' seems to cover a vast number of characteristics of the change factor. Clinical expertise a result of clinical experience is the number one directing force. It influenced a change in the way nurses saw the value of their personal practice. Experience that built this clinical expertise added appreciation of life and death. It gradually tapped sensitive feelings of these nurses for whom acceptance of finiteness of life informed their practice. This demonstrated co-researchers distinct difference from nurses in acute care. By example co-researchers convinced me that by choosing palliative care in mid career they demonstrated exceptional level of empathy for their patients. These nurses coped well with the knowledge that the terminal nature of their patients' condition would invariably result in death and a peaceful end would be the reward for their work.

Experience of patient/nurse connectedness

Experience of patient/nurse connectedness was also behind the manner of how co-researchers faced death and dying day in day out. According to most of these nurses death was not a failure but a relief for their patient. They displayed maturity of experience that underwrote their palliative care competence because of:

- Experience in clinical skills and holistic nursing care
- Humbleness in facing the world and their patients
- Basic empathic nature
- Feeling of privilege at the bedside of dying people
- Constant acceptance of the changing nature of terminal care
- Security in the face of new challenges
- Comfortable with personal mortality
- Open to and accepting of death and dying

These attributes are those of a skilled nurse clinician well into professional practice, and far ahead of that of a novice nurse. These participating nurses demonstrated that experience on various levels influenced the change of their caring ideals and impacted on transferring to palliative caring.

This is nearly all mine—my perspective

All the data from co-researchers left me thinking about what I could add to this rich collection of documented information. Was there anything that my colleagues failed to mention, something that could be specific to me? Then it became clear that these nurses talked about what for them were personal experiences, where no two were exactly the same. They did not call it experience as such, but when reflecting on events in their nursing practice they invariably described something that was memorable. It happened to them and it was knowledge gained through experience.[6]

This prompted me to re-examine my place in the nursing profession. I re-examined why I remained in nursing for fifty years and more. I trained as a nurse because I found that nursing embraced caring as the essential nature of being with vulnerable people because caring is an 'integral part of the nature of nursing'.[7] (Basset 2002, p. 8). At the beginning when I decided to be a nurse and looked through rose-coloured glasses I loved the idea of it, but once I was there and actually doing the work then my eyes were opened to the reality of life in a hospital in the 1950s. During training, as nurse education was known as then, I was subjected to severe military discipline that almost destroyed my caring ambitions. I nearly lost the spirit. All I wanted was to be free of relentless bullying that they called 'training' and give in to the feeling of failure. But what was it that kept me there despite the strict regimented treatment that I endured for three years?

I discovered that I wanted to serve people who needed service, who were in a position of helpless confusion when body function was in a disarray, when illness and suffering turned lives upside down. I decided to remain there and after gaining my certificate as a registered nurse I practiced in various fields. On reaching a high level of clinical experience and practice skills, almost past midlife, I opted for a career in palliative care. The need to be involved in another field where I could make more of a difference gained momentum at my mother's bedside as she died with cancer in a hospice. Mother's care was performed with gentleness and love, and was aimed at both her spiritual welfare and physical comfort. This was the first time I experienced holistic nursing care while I faced the most distressing event of my life—that of the death of my mother. She was treated like the fragile human being she was, with love and respect. At no time was she forced to have treatment she did not want. There was this gentle care and I was looked after as well.

Spending time in that strangely comforting nursing environment I quietly considered my place in the world of nursing. In that hospice

---

6. HG Gadamer *Truth and Method* (London: Continuum Publishing Company, 2000), 257.
7. C Basset, 'Nurses' Pperception of Care and Caring', *International Journal of Nursing Practice*, 8/1 (2002): 8-15, 8.

I woke up to the fact that working in wards with high patient turn over, recording vital signs, handing out medications and changing dressings was no longer satisfying me. I found emotional energies that I wanted to direct towards patients' inner being as well as their physical entity. There was this restless energy within me looking for an outlet. I was not surprised when it came I realized that making a distressed patient comfortable just by adjusting a pillow, moistening a dry lip or just by being there could be reassuring for both of us. I was acutely aware of the change in my caring ideations; there was a progressive transformation in the way I saw my role in nursing. At closer scrutiny it was clear that human metamorphosis takes place when an existing situation is amenable for change, and mine certainly was when I sat with my dying mother.

That was a powerful experience.

There in the hospice at once things felt different. There was not the urgency, the pressure the feverish desire. What was happening to me? I sensed the environment in a different way. All at once I became older and more experienced. I interpreted what I saw with deeper understanding. Did this mean that the culture I was in, my interpretation through deeper awareness and increased knowledge base resulted in a more critical ability of meaning making? Yes, this was the naturally evolving response to life changes. I moved to being more 'inclusive, discriminating, permeable and integrative of experience,'[8] and by dialoguing with peers and co-researchers I became conscious of a change in values of my professional status.

Reflexivity reminded me of personal losses over the years and set me thinking how those losses could be responsible for the development of intense caring attitudes within my nature. This 'gathered hermeneutic significance as [I gave] memory to it'[9] and identified 'experience' as the initiator of memory and sensitivity. This is when I had my 'light bulb' moment and understood the power of experience. It has taken me many words to come to see that ongoing experience is strong enough to change a person's ideals and attitudinal approach. I may have been slow in understanding it but

---

8. MJ Eisen 'Peer-based Professional Development Viewed Through the Lens of Transformative Learning', *Holistic Nursing Practice*, 16/1 (2001): 30-32, 30.
9. M Van Manen, *Researching Lived Experience*, (Ontario: The University of Western Ontario, 1990), 37.

with the help of Gadamer the epiphany happened.[10] Gadamer is very clear in expressing his philosophical views no more so then when he writes about experience. My favourite for some time has been his statement concerning what I understand as the classic explanation of what experience is:

> *The truth of experience always implies an orientation toward new experience.*
>
> *That is why a person who is called experienced has become so not only through experiences but is also open to new experience. The consummation of his experience, the perfection we call "being experienced" does not consist in the fact that someone already knows everything and knows better than anyone else. Rather, the experienced person proves to be, on the contrary, someone who is radically undogmatic; who because of the many experiences he has had and the knowledge he has drawn from them, is particularly well equipped to have new experiences and learn from them.*[11]

Gadamer's exploration of the importance of experience opened my mind to the possibility that nurses' caring approach could be directed by experience as it changes from curing to offering comfort only in end of life situations. This does not happen overnight, often taking several years of clinical and life experience to become confident of the metamorphic wisdom of caring ideals that is the essence of palliative nursing. The two participants in my research who started palliative care without adequate nursing skills soon found that it takes time to digest life and experience, and they got hurt..

---

10. Gadamer *Truth and Method.*
11. Gadamer, Truth and Method, 355.

Chapter 3
Almost the End

Chapter two was the story of not only what my interviewees said but also how that affected me. I developed an increased appreciation for the 'other's' professional practice. It strengthened my earlier belief that in palliative care there are people who are not only competent clinician but are also exceptionally humane people. While I was aware through my practice that caring for dying patients was a special task, I did not know how special until I evaluated it alongside the interview transcripts.

In this the penultimate part of the study I portray the nurse I was searching for and found in myself. Completing the study was a challenging task because auto-ethnography calls for introspective ideation and awareness of the self. It asks for honesty that, on which has to break your heart'[1] to be of value. This study not only embraces professional issues that could be heart breaking but also includes intimate life stories that for me form the soul of nursing dying people. Summary of an auto-ethnographic study is more than words; it is opening up the heart and telling it as it is, even if it hurts.

A profession of emotions

To be a hospice and palliative care nurse is not only a matter of being competent in managing physical symptoms but also to take responsibility for emotional care of the patient at life's end. Acknowledgement and acceptance of psychological pain is of special significance when involved with a person who is dying. It is more

---

1. R Behar, *The vulnerable Observer* (Boston: Beacon Press, 1996), 177.

difficult to face than physical matters. Because of this my study focuses on who the ideal hospice nurse is, and what is that motivates that nurse to be with dying people.

I have discovered that vocation was an intrinsic element in all my participants almost from birth, instilled by parental role modelling and cultural influence. I recognised that interviewees came from backgrounds where values and ethical behaviour came from their home environment, later influencing professional attitude (Sue, Diana). I now know that vocation in early life is not understood as work type of psychological ideation but mainly as awareness of caring for others. This was so in my early childhood as well that did not change for the rest of my life. Awareness for people's pain and frailty was a part of my nature from the time I was a six year-old hospital patient, and was rekindled later at the bedside of my dying father when helpless ineptitude in the face of indescribable suffering urged me to gain skills in helping sick people.

If vocation is a lifelong gift that does not change as indicated by the findings above what then encourages nurses to leave curing in favour of comfort caring of dying patients?

Experience—the heart of transformation

I am comfortable now with the findings that ongoing clinical and life experience is what encourages the nurse to transfer from a curing model of patient care to mainly comfort management of people with life limiting illness. My years in palliative care work and the feedback from nurses I interviewed convinced me that I have come face to face with the research findings of the study. I have no doubt that ongoing learning experience is what primarily inspired nurses to transform their caring approach. Interestingly while observing the palliative care culture I came to the conclusion that much of nursing attributes in the care of dying people are also found in general nursing practice.

My research findings testify to 'clinical experience' as the classic ingredient of therapeutic nursing and a major catalyst for challenging nursing approach to patient care in mid career. This could well explain nurses' transfer to comfort caring when they have accumulated clinical expertise and combined it with rich life experience. There comes a time when it becomes urgent not be the scientific manager of sick people but have time to stabilise existentially distressed patients. Carefully considering interview transcripts I saw characteristic traits that were specific to palliative care nursing. They were unmistakably essential in end of life care without which there was no effective long-term involvement in looking after the welfare of people with life ending problems.

The clinician: an experience-laden story

I was prepared by learning through experience to be the expert clinician. Experience taught me people skills as well as clinical competence and opened my mind to the possibility of transformation that encouraged focusing on the future. German philosopher Immanuel Kant maintains 'there can be no doubt that all our knowledge begins with experience'.[2] Hans Georg Gadamer expends on this by adding that 'experience has its fulfilment not in definitive knowledge but in openness to experience that is made possible by experience itself'.[3] The story of my life sits comfortably with Gadamer because both life and professional experience have influenced my gradual existential transformation. 'The nature of [my] experience was conceived in something that surpasse[d] it',[4] because it was consummated by my philosophical understanding for loss and grief in my own family. While I never thought of being especially profound, intense or philosophical, I knew that I was reflective and thoughtful and was influenced by a strong recall of the past. Memory of my father's death in 1948 bore witness to this in the year of 2004. It was then that for the first time I credited that tragic event with being the precursor for my choice of nursing as a career. That was when I first witnessed death and experienced the painful knowledge of my helplessness in the face of suffering, and I was only fifteen at the time. My Father's death in that post WWII European refugee camp made me grow up suddenly, leaving a legacy of resilience that developed into a committed personality. To help my newly widowed mother I worked as a servant and learnt to ignore pain and discomfort. I

---

2. I Kant, *Immanuel Kant: Critique of pure reason*, translated by M Weigelt and Mueller (London: Peguin, 2007), 37.
3. Gadmaer, Truth and Method, 355.
4. Gadmaer, Truth and Method, 355.

scrubbed floors while suffering high fever during severe asthma attacks, and did that without complaining because I was committed, I promised. All this made me strong and uncomplaining and built the foundation for an ethical work practice.

Migrating to Australia three years later I faced the challenge of a new language and culture that did not deter me from completing a basic nursing course within twelve months. It was not easy living apart from my family in a new country. I was lonely yet that gave me a chance to do extra tasks for patients in the iron lung ward of the post poliomyelitis epidemic in 1951. It was something I loved to do and my solitary life had a meaning. Caring for the less fortunate without expecting remuneration remained a significant feature of my professional life. I later qualified as a registered nurse, married and bore two sons, but nursing continued to play an important role.

For me becoming a nurse was a conscious choice, but palliative care in a way came as a relative surprise being the result of ongoing clinical experience. The desire to change caring roles built up gradually through witnessing futile attempts at resuscitation and the health culture's non-acceptance that healing cannot always be achieved. The world of medicine and nursing cannot send every patient home cured. I began to question some of the attempts at saving lives. Working in a High Dependency Surgical Unit I often observed failing efforts of resuscitation.

Listening to the crash unit doing chest compressions on an already dead patient, and fracturing ribs without restoring life deeply distressed me. I believe that was what initially motivated me to leave the surgical area. My mother's death in the hospice unit of the hospital I worked in added to that desire. Mother dying was the most emotionally intense experience of my adult life. That is when I discovered that there was more to nursing people than concentrating on a medicalised model of care with priorities that often forgot existential matters. The hospice was the first place I came face to face with holistic nursing care where comfort of the patient was the main concern.

The end to my mother's life came peacefully. She had minimal pain, there was care for her spiritual welfare and she did not die alone. Sitting at her bedside I became a part of the caring team. I was never sent away when she was washed, I took over feeding tasks, mouth-care and spoke with her when appropriate. This was a new experience for me because in the general wards visitors are sent out when treatment is in progress. I became impressed with that compassionate nursing care, and with the way none of the staff was intimidated by the impending death of the patient. I was anxious to be a part of it all. Mother spent only ten days in the hospice before she died. Six months later I commenced work there and that is when I recalled Dobratz saying that 'specialty of hospice/palliative care nursing calls for a highly skilled and knowledgeable practitioner'.[5] In a way this underwrote my coming to hospice after thirty years of general nursing, and bore witness to a midlife career change that lasted twenty-two years. Research participants also described their ongoing professional 'experience' as the motivator for their career change.

In hospice work I soon recognised that nurses there had different attitudes towards patient care from that of general hospital areas. Palliative care covered a divergent range of skills that did not focus on life-saving issues. Patients were not prepared for discharge, though it happened sometimes, and even then nursing support for the home environment concentrated on comfort care only. What mattered most in hospice was putting the patient first ahead of bureaucratic demands. To be at the bedside was more important than paper work. I learnt quickly the importance of physical symptom management and to my surprise I already knew a great deal about existential and spiritual caring. I welcomed the opportunity to listen and counsel patient and family in grief. This remains an all-round attitudinal approach on my part that I also found in nurses I interviewed. They all had professional maturity like Rosalie, Liz, Sue, and Mary who agreed that working in hospice was a privilege, as is to give permission for the patient to die. They had love for their patients, and said that they got more from the patients than they gave, and accepted that hospice work helped them to acknowledge their own mortality. Others such as Beth by her own admission liked to care for the patient's body, mind, and spirit. She also preferred to listen, build rapport and understanding.

---

5. M Dobratz, 'Hospice Nursing: Presence, Perspectives and Future Directives', *Cancer Nursing*, 13/2 (1990): 16-22, 16.

There is only one story I found that that speaks of experience as the 'teacher'. As a community palliative carer was Alex who was passionate about her work.

> *George was in his 50s and lived out on a farm a little property, we became very close to him and his wife Anne. We're actually still quite good friends with her and he was just a beautiful-beautiful man. I can remember the very first time I went out to admit him. He was a strong strapping man who had a seizure and was diagnosed with a secondary brain tumor of a lung primary. I went out to the farm to see him because he was basically sent home and told 'you may only have a couple of months to live'. His was a second marriage and I could see that they were so in love and so happy. They were open and honest because they knew he will die eventually but they were going to make the best of the time they had together as they both came out of poor first marriages. His management was quite complicated. Had lots of nausea and pain issues. He was beautiful because you'd go out there and the first thing he wanted to know is how you were and what you were up to before you could get into talking about him. But actually it was his way to forget his illness. 'Tell me what is going on in the outside world? I don't want to talk about my illness. I want to forget about it.' When he had his birthday we all went out there with champagne, we became really good friends. Last year Palliative Care Australia ran a photo story competition. They wanted carers to talk about their dying family member; I knew that Anne would be great to do this. She won that national competition. Told her story about caring for her husband with our help. I actually wrote my story as the nurse. It was lovely to reflect back on it and he was probably the one patient that really ah . . . he was like a real friend.*

Knowledge building—the experience

Experience is one of the most important elements of clinical practice. It is an exciting part of knowledge building. While a great deal of it comes from actual practice in nursing but certain clinical skills are acquired through formal education preceding hands on experience with patients. Yet no matter how much formal education is offered, even at tertiary level, clinical practice remains the best teacher.

Nursing knowledge is constructed of multi shaped post-modern building blocks and is directed by 'caring that accepts and holds safe space for people to seek their own wholeness of being and becoming not only now but [for] the future'.[6] I remember instances where I learnt important lessons through facing unexpected incidents that convinced me that 'the quest for knowledge through creative interpretation of universal experience' played a part in my recognition of true nursing potentials.[7] This 'experiential' knowledge is at the root of human becoming that 'is [a] freely choosing personal meaning in the inter-subjective process of relating [to] value priorities'.[8] (Parse, 1999, p. 6).

Nursing embraces a strong combination of theory and practice where one cannot exist without the other. Clinicians don't often think of this while practising but it is there every day in so many forms as they dip into their knowledge base. I acquired theories around human caring principles while reflecting and questioning myself about the possibility of developing knowledge. Nursing education in my early years did not focus on this. I was not encouraged to be a critical thinker yet I did not take anything for granted. Each nursing situation presented new opportunities to learn from making me an independent thinker and a better clinician. I was there in true presence that was 'intentional human-to-human relating' a foundation for empathic nurse/patient relationship.[9] Each 'caring moment' had the power to transform me by promoting strong praxis awareness. That is when existential ideals assist practical skills resulting in a patient's 'whole person care' While this genre of care, known as holistic nursing, is at a premium for all nursing activities. It is more so in care of terminally ill people.

---

6. J Watson, *Postmodern Nursing and Beyond* (London: Churchill Livingston, 1999), 103.
7. GJ Mitchell, 'The View of Freedom Within the Human Becoming Theory', in *Illuminations*, edited by R Rizzo-Parse (Sudbury: Jones and Bartlett Publishers, 1999), 190.
8. RR Parse, *Illuminations: The Human Becoming Theory in Practice and Research* (Sudbury: Jones and Bartlett Publishers, 1999), 6.
9. Parse, *Illuminations*, 67.

To be a palliative care nurse you must have more

I do not consider this statement too strong because I believe my study demonstrates that looking after people at the end of their life calls for more than what medical science has to offer. When invited into people's end of life struggle there must be an acceptance and understanding of the other's grief, not to be overcome by it, and not seeing death as loss but a natural event of life when the illness can no longer be reversed. The story of Lisa, one of my patients, accurately paints a picture of what I mean.

> *It was at the beginning of a night shift when I met Lisa for the first time. Her story deeply touched me. Just as she was going to give up work and plan a new life with her husband and family—she was diagnosed with pancreatic cancer.*
>
> *Every word she uttered about her experience touched me personally. I did not suffer the disease myself but I endured watching my husband go through Lisa's experience. Steven died with pancreatic cancer also.*
>
> *I did not share this with Lisa initially. Later in the night she talked of her limited future and was uncertain where she should die, hospice or home." How can I die at home letting my husband remain there with memories of me?"*
>
> *This gave me the opening to tell her that I respected my husband's wish to die at home and I said that this did not affect me in any adverse way. On the contrary it pleased me that he died in the home he loved, the home he put finishing touches to as he slowly weakened. Lisa's reaction was a revelation of how appropriate sharing of an experience can be healing. It could open the door to questions that help. Lisa repeatedly said how good it is to hear of another person who suffered an identical disease; it helped her see her future.*
>
> *I was reluctant to go on, but she insisted. Lisa asked me about how Steven progressed and her questions directed my answers. I spoke positively about the last weeks during which he managed very well.*

> Lisa thanked me and said how honest information was what she has been looking for. She maintained how much better she felt after hearing that she would be able to walk and talk and her appearance will be acceptable to her husband and children. She began to cry. That according to her was also a new experience because she as a rule found it difficult to cry.
>
> The week following I was not working and read Lisa's obituary in the local paper. I could hardly believe it; only a few nights ago I was with her and told her I have time. I remained with her because I had a feeling she still had a lot to say. Only a week before her death I listened and indulged in self-disclosure, something I rarely do. This was so appropriate though as Lisa maintained that she never got the answers she looked for until she met me. And now she is dead. Her main concerns were around being in reasonable control to the end. As she had identically presenting cancer as Steven, I could safely tell her that she will be able to talk, walk, and be with her family to the end. She was also worried about her appearance that could scare her children. Well she looked good the night she shared her concerns only a few days before her death.

This story has much of the existential features that make up the palliative care experience. There was recognition of my personal pain that in fact helped to calm Lisa's distress about the place of death. My comfort with openly speaking about the death of my husband contributed to both Lisa's and my expanded consciousness and 'patterning' that looks at the sick person not as a disease process but as someone with an embodied disturbance that offers humans to evolve on a higher level of complexity. Rhythmical patterning that reveals and conceals allowed me to connect and separate at the same time, important when nursing dying people. To function as a hospice worker the nurse must closely identify with the patient initially but have the ability to 'let go' after the patient dies. As a long-term hospice nurse I can offer not only my competency of practice in end of life caring but share valuable emotional experience in loss situations.

One of the critical questions the hospice nurse faces is 'how can you do this work?' I mention this because the answer often opens up the matter of goal setting. Palliative care's goal is not curing or actually promoting physical healing but it looks at emotional healing and physical comfort caring. My answer to people questioning me was inevitably one that speaks to these aspects of nursing. But I also add that achieving these aims leave me with comfort of having done a job well. Seeing grieving relatives at the time of a comfortable family death is my remuneration.

The palliative care nurse learns to cope with difficult to understand situations with motivation and commitment. As such I confidently say that altruism, dedication, caring, trust and loyalty have been the elements of the ultimate commitment of palliative caring. In some this was built on a personal memory of death in early life. In others open honest relationship within the family unit of caring and sharing encouraged a vocational attitude. I also detected sensitivity to life matters and love for those who are weaker, but humbleness and gentle caring were the most outstanding qualities of most nurses I interviewed. While you may say that these attributes could be seen in other nursing specialties but because palliative care/hospice nursing is mostly concerned with interpersonal existential issues at a time when death is imminent, it calls for special attributes by its nurses. Comfort with personal mortality and acceptance of the inevitability of the patient's death are specific qualities in nurses who opt for palliative care. Death is a natural part of living and if a nurse, while competent in clinical care, does not accept this she will suffer burnout along the way, as did Eve and Melanie.

It is not easy to witness life ending situations day in day out. The nurse contemplating palliative care as a career path needs to find her goal setting ideals, examine personal attitudes to death and dying and have solid clinical skills base with basic love of people and their existential issues.

End of the story

I introduced the study with a letter to my son, a consulting oncologist, who on reading it was taken aback somewhat but agreed to the idea of its inclusion with some enthusiasm.

In the first volume I described my experience with the death of my Mother, Father and Husband whom I nominated as guiding spirits for this study.

I continued this with examining scholarly issues of data gathering, methodology and philosophical aspects.

In the first chapters of this second volume I walked the trail with expert palliative care nurses to find where we came from as we ride on the train of auto-ethnography of person and culture. These parts paid homage to Carolyn Ellis' idea of meta-auto-ethnography.[10] Like Ellis I spent many hours going back and forth reading stories of nurses I interviewed continuously coming across similarities to my palliative care ideals. Each transcript holds meaning for my belief that palliative care requires special qualities in those who practice it. Combining the personal and cultural aspects of end of life experience in patient care I came up with succinct answers to what is behind nurses' motivation to transfer mid career to palliative care.

I continued this by examining what I learnt by searching and reflecting on my professional integrity as a hospice nurse and weighing it up alongside other practitioners in the care of dying people. I found that career transformation was an individual choice of the experienced clinician and it mainly occurred in mid career for most nurses in this study, and it was an established fact for me.

I gradually came to the conclusion that to become palliative carers, nurses require *clinical expertise* before engaging in caring for people with life limiting illness. This generally means an extended period in acute and speciality areas. Other attributes include ability to *engage with sick patients* and having ongoing *life experience* that promotes a non-judgemental attitude. As I evaluate my transfer to palliative care it becomes clear that 'experience' in its many forms was responsible for my skill development for the care of people who will not recover from their disease processes. I readily accepted the fact that my patients in the hospice would die sooner than later and consequently I concentrated on whole person care. This included the spirit and emotions, alongside that of the physical body. For me this was the essence of palliative care.

I also found that coming in contact with often futile efforts to keep dying patients alive was one of the significant motives for not only me but also for co-researchers to transfer to comfort caring only. These nurses having experienced frustration in Intensive Care situations spoke of their distress of dying patients with terminal diseases being kept alive without a level of comfort. This is identical to how I

---

10. C Ellis, *Revision: Autoethnographic Reflections on Life and Work,* (Wlnut Cross: Left Coast Press, 2009).

responded to futile resuscitation of patients in the high dependency surgical unit I worked in for seven years.

This was by no means the only reason for nurses' career transformation. Some were inspired by a death in the family, others wished for an opportunity to practice holistic patient care, but a common bond among the nurses I interviewed was their belief in the spirituality of their patients. In this context spirituality does not strictly mean 'religion', it means the whole gamut of human nature that is living a life in an independent way.

Findings of my study at the finish came up with attributes that best describe palliative care nurses' qualities, and are essential building blocks of nursing patients with time limiting illnesses. These qualities are in part innate and personal but a number of the following attributes are acquired by experience at the bedside of sick patients. I find them valid and a true picture of my and co-researchers' belief system

- Comfort with death and dying
- Comfort with personal mortality
- Intensive caring
- Companionship with suffering
- Emotional strength
- Non-judgmental understanding

In essence the principle dynamics affecting nurses to take on palliative care according to this study is that certain well qualified experienced nurses are not comfortable with some general nursing areas' disregard for the holistic care of terminally ill patients. This is demonstrated by interview results where a number of co-researchers talk of the way they felt comfortable in hospice units where there was time for whole person care of their patients.

My research informants conformed to a pattern of expertise that indicates several points. The strongest one is that competency in nursing skills arrived at by clinical experience in over all patient care is what develops essential attributes for effective palliative care. By this I mean that clinical nursing competence in physical and existential care is the corner stone for end of life nursing of patients. My research indicates that a nurse generally achieves this in mid career. That is when personal emotional strength seems to be most available to the nursing practitioner. An understanding and acceptance of death as a necessary part of living is imperative to the palliative care nurse. Interestingly, she will also doubtless have a healthy awareness of personal mortality issues. Palliative care is not a simple career choice entered into lightly. However, my research indicates that it becomes a long-term commitment when taken on board at the appropriate career stage.

To end my story I would like to add a powerful comment on Palliative Care by the 2013 Senior Australian of the year, Emeritus Palliative Care Professor Ian Maddox, in his address to the 2009 International Palliative Care Conference in Perth Western Australia:

> *Palliative Care offers an example of what can be won from an anxious situation of impending demise. It acknowledges a hope founded in love and courage and patience rather than desperate survival, and so it proclaims a still, small message for a terminal world.*

Epilogue
A final request

Dear Boys,

I am getting closer to the point every one reaches, no matter how fortunate or fit and well. Life must come to an end we are not meant to live forever. Understanding this is easy, but accepting it is a little more difficult. As a rather ordinary human being I have a healthy mistrust of what could be behind that mysterious door leading to the other existence—no longer a physical one. I think about it quite often, not with panic or fear, but curiosity. What I am dreading though is the uncertainty of the dying process. If you have scanned this document you would know that my knowledge of dying is extensive. Having witnessed all manner of ending life I want to ensure that if it is at all possible I should have a comfortable one. That is why this letter is the other bookend of my thesis that asks for a favour from both of you. Please be there to see that my wishes are carried out as far as humanly possible. Should it be that I am suffering from an incurable illness, just let me die my way.

Both of you are familiar with my legal instructions as far as treatment issues go, but in addition I have a request for simple palliative nursing and medical care when I am no longer strong enough to ask for it myself should I have a terminal illness.

Please make sure that physicians with their cold stethoscopes, who don't understand what I am going through, will be kept away from me. I want a doctor who sits at my bed and only uses his ears to listen for my breathing while holding my hand.

When I refuse food or nourishing drinks just suggest ice chips or sips of cold water. I may be nauseated.

Do get the doctors to prescribe adequate pain and nausea relief, not just write up a 'give when necessary' order. I don't want to rely on having to ask for medication for distressing symptoms. Let me be treated by doctors who know their craft.

Please tell the nurses that I only want to be moved when it is absolutely necessary and even then not when I am comfortably sleeping. I know it is difficult not to comply with the two to three hourly turn routines, but I will be dying soon so why do a few red spots on my body matter?

Please ask the nurses to use only water to clean and moisten my mouth once I cannot drink any more. Expensive odorous medical drops only will make me even more nauseous.

When it comes to the matter of toileting, a catheter in my bladder and a large pad may be the way to go. Please no extensive bowel intervention at the very end. I don't mind if I go to heaven with a full rectum.

And please have some classical music playing in the background—I love Phillip Glass.

This may seem rather simplistic but believe me, I learnt by experience to provide the best and what I ask for in this letter is the 'best'. Doctors and nurses tend to get carried away with their importance and forget that their patient might want to have a say in how she dies. This letter with your help will ensure my peaceful end, and at the same time put a full stop to this study.

All my love,

Mum

Bibliography

Aindow, A & Brook, L 2008, 'Essential medicines list for children', viewed 23.5.2012, http://www.who.int/selection_medicines/committees/subcommittee/2/palliative pdf

Agrimson, LB 2008, 'Spiritual crisis: a concept analysis', in *Journal of Advanced Nursing*, vol. 65, no. 2, pp. 454-461.

Alford, EF 2006, 'Only a piece of meat: one patient's reflection on her eight-day hospital visit', in *Qualitative Inquiry*, vol. 12, no. 3, pp. 596-620.

Anderson, L 2006,'Analytic autoethnography', in *Journal of Contemporary Ethnography*, vol. 35, no. 4, pp. 373-395.

Authier, P 2004, 'Being present – the choice that re-instills caring', in *Nursing Administration Quarterly*, vol. 28, no. 4, pp. 276-279.

Barbato-Gaydos, L 2004, 'The living end', in *Journal of Hospice and Palliative Care*, vol. 6, no.1, pp. 17-26.

Bartleet, BL 2009, 'Behind the baton: exploring autoethnographic writing in a musical context', in *Journal of Contemporary Ethnography,* vol. 38, no. 6, pp. 713-733.

Basset, C 2002, 'Nurses' perception of care and caring', in *International Journal of Nursing Practice*, vol. 8, no.1, pp. 8-15.

Bauby, JD 2000, *The diving bell and the butterfly,* Harper Perennial, London.

Behar, R 1996, *'The vulnerable observer'*, Beacon Press, Boston.

Benner, P 2001, *From novice to expert: excellence and power in clinical nursing practice,* Prentice Hall, Upper Saddler River, N.J.

Benner, P & Wruebel, J (eds) 1989, *The Primacy of caring,* Addison Wesley Publishing Company, Menlo Park, California.

Berger, L 2001, 'Inside out: narrative autoethnography as a path toward rapport', in *Qualitative Inquiry*, vol. 7, no. 4, pp. 504-518.

Berzoff, J & Silverman, PR (eds) 2004, *Living with dying: handbook for end-of-life healthcare practitioners*, Columbia University Press, New York.

Bochner, AP 1994, 'Perspectives on inquiry II', in *Handbook of Interpersonal Communication*, 2nd edn, (eds) ML Knapp & GR Miller, Sage Publications, Thousand Oaks, California.

Bochner, A 2001, 'Narrative Virtues', in *Qualitative Inquiry*, vol. 7, no. 2, pp. 131-158.

Bochner, AP 2007, 'Notes toward an ethics of memory in autoethnographic inquiry', in *Ethical Futures in Qualitative Research*, (eds) NK Denzin & MD Giardia, Left Coast Press Inc., Walnut Creek, CA94596.

Bochner, AP 2012, 'Suffering happiness', in *Qualitative Communication Research*, vol. 1, no. 2, pp. 209-229.

Bochner, AP & Ellis C1996, 'Introduction', in *Composing ethnography: alternative forms of qualitative writing*, (eds) C Ellis & AP Bochner, Alta Mira Press, Walnut Creek, California.

Bochner, AP & Ellis, C (eds) 2002, *Ethnographically Speaking: Autoethnography, Literature and Aesthetics*, Alta Mira Press, Walnut Creek, California.

Bolton, SC 2000, 'Who cares? offering emotion work as a "gift" in the nursing labour process', in *Journal of Advanced Nursing*, vol. 32, no. 3, pp. 580-6.

Bradshaw, A 1994, *Lighting the lamp: the spiritual dimensions of nursing care*, Scutari, London.

Bradshaw, A 1996, 'The spiritual dimension of hospice: the secularisation of an ideal', in *Social Science and Medicine*, vol. 43, no. 3, pp. 409-419.

Bradshaw, A 1999, 'The virtue of nursing: the covenant of care', *Journal of Medical Ethics*, vol. 25, no. 6, pp. 477- 481.

Bradshaw, A 2012, 'Gadamer's two Horizons: listening to the voices in nursing history', in *Nursing Inquiry*, vol. 195, no. 9, pp. 518-522.

Brajtman, S 2003, 'The impact on the family of terminal restlessness and its management', in *Palliative Medicine*, vol. 17, pp. 454-460.

Bruni, N 2002, 'Crisis of visibility: ethical dilemmas of autoethnographic research', in *Qualitative Research Journal*, vol 2, no. 1, pp. 24-32.

Buechner, F 1993, *Wishful thinking: a seeker's ABC*, Harper Collins Publishers, New York.

Buber, M 1958, *I and thou*, Charles Scribner's Sons, New York.

Buber, M 1998, *Knowledge of man: selected essays*, Educational Theory, Humanity Books, New York.

Burnard, P 2007, 'Seeing the psychiatrist: an autoethnographic account', in *Journal of research in nursing*, vol. 14, pp. 808-814.

Carper, BA 1978, 'Practice oriented theory: part 1, Fundamental patterns of knowing in nursing, *Advances in Nursing Science*, vol. 1 no. 1, pp. 13-23, in *Theoretical Nursing: Development and Progress*, 4th edn, AI Meleis, 2007.

Chalmers, David J (1995), 'Explaining consciousness: the "hard problem"', in *Journal of Consciousness Studies*, vol. 2, no. 3, pp. 200-219.

Chang, H 2008, *Autoethnography as method*, Left Coast Press, INC. 1630 North Main Street #400, Walnut Creek, CA 94596.

Charles, LL 2009, 'My nine lives as an academic: narratives of identity storied by a platinum-enhanced brain', in *Qualitative Inquiry*, vol. 15, no. 10, pp. 1592-1611.

Charmaz, K & Mitchell, RG Jnr 1997, 'The myth of silent authorship: self, substance, and style in ethnographic writing', in *Reflexivity and voice*, (ed) R. Hertz, Sage Publications, Thousand Oaks, California.

Charmaz, K 1999, 'Stories of suffering: subjective tales and research narratives', in *Qualitative Health Research*, vol. 9, no. 3, pp. 362-382.

Charon, JM 2004, *Symbolic Interactionism*, 8th edn, Pearson Prentis Hall, Upper Saddle River, New Jersey 07458.

Chase, SE 2001, 'Response to "The concept of nursing presence: state of the science"', in *Scholarly Inquiry for Nursing Practice: An International Journal*, vol. 15, pp. 323-327.

Chase, SE 2005, 'Narrative Inquiry' in *The Sage Handbook of Qualitative Research*, 3rd edn, (eds) NK Denzin & YS Lincoln, Sage Publications, Thousand Oaks, California.

Clarke, J 2006, 'A discussion paper about 'meaning' in the nursing literature on spirituality: an interpretation of meaning as 'ultimate concern' using the work of Paul Tillich', in *Nursing Studies,* vol. 43, pp. 915-921.

Clark, D 1996, 'Interview with Colin Murray Parkes', *Hospice History Program,* viewed on May 18, 2011, at 5.28 pm, http://www.hospice-history.org.uk

Clark D 2000, 'Total pain: the work of Cicely Saunders and the hospice movement', *APS Bulletin,* vol. 10, no. 4, viewed on 14.05.2011, http://www.ampainsoc.org/library/bulletin/jul00/hist.1.htm

Clark, D 2002, 'Between hope and acceptance: the medicalisation of dying', in *British Medical Journal,* vol. 324, no. 7342, pp. 905-907.

Clark, TW 2002, 'Is there an observing self?' *Science and Consciousness Review,* Viewed on 10.9. 2010, http://sciconrev.org/2004/02/is-there-an-observing-self

Coffey, A 1999, *The ethnographic self,* Sage Publications, London EC2A4PU.

Cohen, JB, 2004, 'Late for school: stories for transformation in an adult education program', in *Journal of Transformative Education,* vol. 2, no. 3, pp. 242-252.

Colaizzi, PF 1978, 'Psychological research as the phenomenologist views it', in *Existential-phenomenological alternatives for psychology,* (eds) RS Valle & M King, Oxford University Press, New York.

Coles, R 1989, *The call of stories: teaching and the moral imagination,* Boston: Houghton Mifflin.

Collins, M 1991, *Adult Education as Vocation,* Routledge, New York.

Covington, H 2005, 'Caring presence: providing a safe space for patients', in *Holistic Nursing Practice,* vol. 19, no. 4, pp. 169-172.

Cowling III, RW 1999, 'Unitary transformative nursing science: potentials for transcending dichotomies', in *Nursing Science Quarterly,* vol. 12, no. 2, pp. 132-137.

Cramer, LD, McCorkle, R, Cherlin, E, Johnson-Huzeler, R & Bradley, EH 2003, 'Nurses' attitudes and practice related to hospice care', in *Journal of Nursing Scholarship,* vol. 35, no. 3, pp. 249-255.

Cranton, P & Roy, M 2003, 'When the bottom falls out of the bucket', in *Journal of Transformative Education,* vol. 1, no. 2, pp. 86-98.

Cranton, P 2006, *Understanding and promoting transformative learning*, 2nd edn, Jossey-Bass, San Francisco CA.

Crawford, L 1996, Personal ethnography, in *Communication Monographs*, vol. 63, p. 158.

Dawson, J 2005, 'A history of vocation: tracing a keyword of work, meaning, and moral purpose', in *Adult Education Quarterly*, vol. 55, no. 3. pp. 220-231.

Denzin, NK 1992, 'The many faces of emotionality: reading persona', in *Investigating subjectivity*, (eds) C Ellis & MG Flaherty, Sage Publications, Newbury Park, London, New Delhi.

Denzin, NK 1999, 'Interpretive ethnography', vol. 28, no. 5, pp. 510-519.

Denzin, NK & Lincoln, YS (eds) 2000, *Handbook of Qualitative Research*, 2nd edn, Sage Publication, Thousand Oaks, California.

Denzin, NK & Lincoln, YS (eds) 2005, *The Sage Handbook of Qualitative Research*, 3rd edn, Sage Publications, Thousand Oaks, California.

Devine, A 2001, 'Narrating nursing jurisdiction: "atrocity stories" and "boundary work"', in *Symbolic Interaction*, vol. 24, no. 1, pp. 1-27.

Dik, BJ & Duffy, RD 2008, 'Calling and vocation at work: definition and prospects for research and practice', *The Counselling Psychologist*, vol. 37, no. 3, pp. 424-450.

Dobratz, M 1990, 'Hospice nursing: presence, perspectives and future directives', in *Cancer Nursing*, vol. 13, no. 2, pp. 16-22.

Dobratz, MC 2006, 'Enriching the portrait: methodological triangulation of life-closing theory', in *Advances in Nursing Science*, vol. 29, no. 3, pp. 260-270.

Dreyfus, H & Dreyfus, S 1986, *Mind over machine*, New York: Free Press.

Doyle, D, Hanks, G & MacDonald, N 2003, 'Introduction', in *The Oxford Textbook of Palliative Medicine*, 2nd edn, (eds) D. Doyle, G. Hanks & N. MacDonald, Oxford University Press, Oxford.

Duldt-Battey, BW 2004, 'Humanism, nursing, communication, and holistic care: a position paper on line, viewed 7.7.2011, http://www.samuelmerritt.edu/depts/nursing/duldt

DuBoulay, S 1984, *Cecily Saunders: Founder of the Modern Hospice Movement*, Hodder and Stoughton, London, Sydney, Auckland, Toronto.

Edvardsson, JD, Sandman, P & Rasmussen, BH 2003, 'Meaning of giving touch in the care of older patients: becoming a valuable person and professional', in *Journal of Clinical Nursing*, vol. 12, pp. 601-609.

Edvardsson, D & Street, A 2007, 'Sense or no-sense: the nurse as embodied ethnographer', in *International Journal of Nursing Practice*, vol. 13. pp. 24-32.

Edwards, SD 1998, 'The art of nursing', *Nursing Ethics*, vol. 5, no. 5, pp. 393-400.

Effken, JA 2007, 'The informational basis for nursing intuition: philosophical underpinnings', in *Nursing Philosophy*, vol. 8, pp. 187-200.

Eisen, MJ 2001, 'Peer-based professional development viewed through the lens of transformative learning', in *Holistic Nursing Practice*, vol. 16, no. 1, pp. 30-32.

Elias, D 1997, 'Its time to change our minds', *ReVision*, p. 26.

Elias, JI 2003, 'Reflections on the vocation of a religious teacher', in *Religious Education, The Official Journal of the Religious Education Association*, vol. 98, no. 3, pp. 297-310.

Elligson, L 1998, '"Then you know how I feel": Empathy, identification, and reflexivity in fieldwork', in *Qualitative Inquiry*, vol. 4, no. 4, pp. 492-514.

Elligson, LL 2006, 'Embodied knowledge: writing researchers' bodies into qualitative health research', in *Qualitative Health Research*, vol. 10, no. 2, pp. 298-310.

Ellis, C 1991, 'Sociological introspection and emotional experience', in *Symbolic Interaction*, vol.14, no. 1, pp. 23-50.

Ellis, C 2000,' Creating criteria: an ethnographic short story', in *Qualitative Inquiry*, vol. 6, no. 2, pp. 273-277.

Ellis, C 2001, 'Being real: moving towards social change', in *Qualitative Studies in Education*, vol. 13, no. 4, pp. 399-406.

Ellis, C 2004, *'The ethnographic I'*, Alta Mira Press, Walnut Creek, Lanham, New York, Oxford.

Ellis, C 2007,'Telling secrets, revealing lives: relational ethics in research with intimate others', in *Qualitative Inquiry*, vol. 13, no. 1, pp. 1-14.

Ellis, C 2009, *Revision: autoethnographic reflections on life and work*, Left Coast Press Inc. 1630 North Main Street, #400 Walnut Creek, California 94596.

Ellis, C & Bochner, A 2000, Autoethnography, personal narrative, reflexivity, in *Handbook of Qualitative Research* 2nd edn, (eds) NK Denzin & YS Lincoln, Sage Publications, Thousand Oaks, California.

Ellis, C & Bochner, AP 2006, 'Analysing analytic autoethnography: an autopsy', in *Journal of Contemporary Ethnography*, vol. 35, no. 4, pp. 429-449.

Ellis, C & Flaherty, M (eds) 1992, *Investigating subjectivity: research on lived experience*, Sage Publications, Newbury Park, London, New Delhi.

Ellis, C, Kiesinger & Tillman-Healy, L 1997, 'Interactive interviewing: talking about emotional experience', in *Reflexivity and voice*, (ed) R Hertz, Sage Publications, Thousand Oaks, California.

Endo, E, Myahara, T, Suzuki, S & Ohmasa, T 2005, 'Partnering of researcher and practising nurses for transformative nursing', in *Nursing Science Quarterly*, vol. 18, no. 2, pp. 138-145.

Erikson, E 1987, 'The way of looking at things', in *Personality and personal growth*, 3rd edn, (eds) J Fadiman & R Frager, Harper Collins College Publishers, 10 East 53rd, Street, New York, 1994.

Estes, PC 1992, '*Women who run with the wolves*', Griffin Paperbacks, Watson Avenue, Netley, South Australia.

Etherington, K 2004, *Becoming a Reflexive Researcher*, Atheneum Press, Gateshead, Tyne and Wear.

Evans, JM & Hallet, CE 2007, 'Living with dying: a hermeneutic phenomenological study of the work of hospice nurses', in *Journal of Clinical Nursing*, vol. 16, pp. 742-751.

Fink, R & Gates, R 2006, 'Pain assessment' in *Textbook of palliative care*, 2nd edn, (eds) BR Ferrel & N Coyle, Oxford University Press.

Fingfeld-Connet, D 2006, 'Meta-synthesis of presence in nursing', in *Journal of Advanced Nursing*, vol. 55, no. 6, pp. 708-714.

Foster, K, McAllister, M & O'Brien, L 2006, 'Extending the boundaries: autoethnography as an emergent method in mental health nursing research', in *International Journal of Mental Health Nursing*, vol. 15, pp. 44-53.

Foster, E 2007, *Communicating at the end of life: finding magic in the mundane*, Lawrence Erlbaum Associates, Publishers, Mahwah, New Jersey, London.

Fredriksson, L 1999, 'Modes of relating in a caring conversation: a research synthesis on presence, touch and listening', in *Journal of Advanced Nursing*, vol. 30, no. 5, pp. 1167-1176.

Freshwater, D (ed) 2002, *Therapeutic Nursing*, Sage Publications, London, Thousand Oaks, New Delhi.

Frankl, V 1995, *Man's Search for Meaning*, Hodder and Stroughton, Seven Oaks California.

Gadamer, H.G 2000, *Truth and Method*, Continuum Publishing Company, New York.

Gadamer, H.G 1996, *Enigma of Health*, Stanford University Press, Stanford California.

Gastmans, C 1999, 'Care as a moral attitude', in *Nursing Ethics*, vol. 6, no. 3, pp. 214-223.

Gearity, BT & Mertz, N 2012, 'From "bitch" to "mentor": a doctoral student's story of self-change and mentoring', in *The Qualitative Report*, vol. 17, article 59, pp. 1-27, viewed 10 July 20, http://www.nova.edu/ssss/QR/QR17/gearity.pdf

Geertz, C 2000, *The interpretation of cultures*, Basic Books, New York.

Goodall, HL jnr. 2000, '*Writing the new ethnography*', Alta Mira Press, Walnut Creek, New York, Oxford.

Gordon, M 2011, 'Listening as embracing the other: Martin Buber's philosophy of dialogue', in *Educational Theory*, vol. 61, no. 2, pp. 207-219.

Guba, EG & Lincoln, YS 1994,' Competing paradigms in qualitative research', in *Handbook of qualitative research*, (eds) NK Denzin & YS Lincoln, Sage Publications, Thousand Oaks, California.

Gubrium, JF & Holstein, JA (eds) 1997, *The new language of qualitative method*, New York: Oxford University Press.

Gubrium, JF & Holstein, JA (eds) 2001, *"Handbook of Interview Research"*, Sage Publications, Thousand Oaks, London, New Delhi.

Gubrium, JF & Holstein, JA (eds) 2003, *Postmodern interviewing*, Sage Publications, Thousand Oaks, California.

Hardy, S, Titchen, A & Manley, K 2007, 'Patient narratives in the investigation and development of nursing practice expertise: a potential for transformation', in *Nursing Inquiry,* vol. 14, no. 1, pp. 80-88.

Haworth, SK & Dluhy, N M 2001, 'Holistic symptom management: modelling the interaction phase', in *Journal of Advanced Nursing,* vol. 36, no. 2, pp. 302-310.

Hertz, R (ed) 1997, *Reflexivity and voice,* Sage Publications, Thousand Oaks, California 91320.

Hermann, CP 2001, 'Spiritual needs of dying patients: a qualitative study', in *Oncology nurses forum,* vol. 28, no 1.

Hill Bailey, P &Tilley, S 2002, 'Story telling and the interpretation of meaning in qualitative research', in *Journal of Advanced Nursing,* vol. 38, no. 6, pp. 574-583.

Holland-Wade, G 1998, 'A concept analysis of personal transformation', in *Journal of Advanced Nursing,* vol. 28, no. 4, p.713.

Holman-Jones, S 2005, 'Autoethnography: making the personal political' in *Handbook of Qualitative Research,* 3rd edn, (eds) NK Denzin & YS Lincoln, Sage Publications, Thousand Oaks, London, New Delhi.

Hopkinson, JB, Hallettt, CE & Luker, KA 2003, 'Caring for dying people in hospitals', in *Journal of Advanced Nursing,* vol. 44 no. 5, pp. 525.

Hospice Education Institute on line viewed 15.05.2011, http://www.hospiceworld.org/history.htm

Hupcey, JE, Penrod, J, Morse, JM & Mitcham, C 2001, 'An exploration and advancement of the concept of trust', in *Journal of Advanced Nursing,* vol. 36, no. 2, pp. 282-293.

Hutchings, D 1997, 'The hardiness of hospice nurses', in *The American Journal of Hospice and Palliative Care,* May-June, pp. 110-113.

Hutchinson, TA (ed) 2011, *Whole person care,* Springer, New York, Dordrec Heidelberg, London.

Jablonski, A & Wyatt, KG 2005, 'A model for identifying barriers to effective symptom management at the end of life', in *Journal of Hospice and Palliative Nursing,* vol. 7, no. 1.

Johns, C 2001.'Reflective practice: revealing the [he]art of caring', in *International Journal of Nursing Practice,* vol. 7, pp. 237-245.

Johns, C 2004, *'Being mindful, easing suffering, reflections on palliative care',* Jessica Kingsley Publishers, London and New York.

Johns, C 2006, *'Engaging reflection in practice'*, Blackwell Publishing, Oxford.

Johns, C 2010, *Guided reflection: a narrative approach to advancing professional practice*, Blackwell Publishing, Oxford.

Johns, C & Freshwater, (eds) 2005, *Transforming nursing through reflective practice*, 2nd edn, Blackwell Publishing, Oxford.

Johnston, B 2002, 'Overview of nursing developments in palliative care', in *Palliative care: the nursing role*, (eds) J Lugton & M Kidlen, Churchill Livingston.

Johnston, B & LN Smith 2005, 'Nurses and patients' perceptions of expert palliative nursing care' *Journal of Advanced Nursing,* vol. 54, no. 6, pp. 700-709.

Johnstone, MJ 1999, 'Reflective topical autobiography: an under utilized interpretive research in nursing', in *Collegian,* vol. 6, no. 1, pp. 24-29.

Kalmbach-Phillips, D, Harris, G, Legard-Larson, M & Higgins, K 2009, 'Trying on being: four women's journey(s) in feminist post-structural theory', in *Qualitative Inquiry,* vol. 15, pp. 1455-1479.

Kallstrom-Karlsson, IL, Ehnfors, M & Ternested, BM 2008, 'Five nurses' experiences of hospice care in a long-term perspective', in *Journal of Hospice and Palliative Nursing,* vol. 10, no. 4, pp. 224-232.

Kant, I 2007, *Immanuel Kant: Critique of pure reason,* trans. M Weigelt, Peguin, London.

Kehoe, MH 2006, ' Embodiment of hospice nurses: a meta-synthesis of qualitative studies', in *Journal of Hospice and Palliative Nursing,* vol. 8, no. 3, pp. 137-146.

Kendall, S 2007, 'Witnessing tragedy: nurses' perceptions of caring for patients with cancer', in *International Journal of Nursing Practice,* vol. 13, pp. 111-120.

Kidd, J & Finlayson, M 2009, 'When needs must: interpreting autoethnographical stories', in *Qualitative Inquiry,* vol.15, no. 6, pp. 34-50.

King, L & Appleton, JV 1997, 'Intuition: a critical review of the research and rhetoric', in *Journal of Advanced Nursing,* vol. 26, pp. 194-202.

King, C 2006, 'Nausea and vomiting', in *Textbook of Palliative Nursing* 2nd edn, (eds) BR Ferrel & N Coyle, Oxford University Press.

Kincheloe, JL & McLaren, P 2000, 'Rethinking critical theory and qualitative research, in *Handbook of Qualitative Research*, 2nd edn, (eds) NK Denzin & YS Lincoln, Sage Publications, Thousand Oaks, California.

Knight, K 2009, 'In his time of dying: communication and silence in family illness and death', in *Qualitative Inquiry*, vol. 15, no. 10, pp. 1612-1624.

Kobasa SC 1979, 'Stressful life events, personality and health: an inquiry into hardiness', in *Journal of Personal & Social Psychology*, vol. 37 pp. 34-37.

Kolker A 1996,'Thrown overboard: the human cost of health care rationing', in *Composing ethnography*, (eds) C Ellis & A Bochner, Alta Mira Press, Walnut Creek California.

Kottow, MH 2001, 'Between caring and curing', in *Nursing Philosophy*, vol. 2, pp. 53-61.

Kosowski, MM & Roberts, W 2003, 'When protocols are not enough: intuitive decision making by novice nurse practitioners', in *Journal of Holistic Nursing*, vol. 21, no. 1, pp. 52-72.

Krakauer, EL, Penson, RT, Truog, RD, King, LA, Charner, BA & Lynch, JR 2000, 'Sedation for intractable distress of a dying patient: acute palliative care and the principle of double effect', in *The Oncologist*, vol. 5, pp. 53-62.

Kunyk, D & Olson, JK 2001, 'Clarification and conceptualisation of empathy', in *Journal of Advanced Nursing*, vol. 35, no. 3, pp. 317-325.

Kubler-Ross, E 1969, *On death and dying*, Tavistock Publications, London.

Kvale, S 1996, *"InterViews"*, Sage Publications, Thousand Oaks, London, New Delhi.

Laskowski, C & Pellicore, K 2002, 'The wounded healer archetype: application to palliative care practice', in *American Journal of Hospice and Palliative Care*, vol. 19, no. 6, pp. 403-407.

Lavoie, M, Blondeau, D, & De Koninck 2008, 'The dying person: an existential being until the end of life', in *Nursing Philosophy*, vol. 9, pp. 89-97.

Liaschenko, J & Peter, E 2003,' Nursing ethics and conceptualisation of nursing: profession, practice and work', in *Journal of Advance Nursing*', vol. 46, no. 5, pp. 488-495.

Lindseth, A & Norberg, A 2004, 'A phenomenological hermeneutical method for researching lived experience', in *Scandinavian Journal of Caring Sciences,* vol. 18, pp. 145-153.

Linge, DE (ed) 1997, *Philosophical Hermeneutics-Hans Georg Gadamer,* University of California Press, Berkeley, Los Angeles, London.

Lundmark, M 2007, 'Vocation in theology-based nursing theories', in *Nursing Ethics,* vol. 14, no. 6, pp. 767-780.

Maatta, SM 2006, 'Closeness and distance in the nurse-patient relations: the relevance of Edith Stein's concept of empathy', in *Nursing Philosophy,* vol. 7, pp. 3-10.

Macnish, K 2002,' Palliative nursing', in *Palliative care for people with cancer,* 3rd edn, (eds) J Penson, & RA Fisher, Arnold Publishers, London, New York, New Delhi.

Magno, JB 2011, International Association for Hospice and Palliative Care, viewed at 11.06.2011, http://www.hospicecare.com/Bio/jb_magno.htm

Manias, E, Botti, M, Bucknall, M, 2002, 'Observation of pain assessment and management – the complexities of clinical practice', in *Journal of Clinical Practice,* vol. 11, pp. 724-733.

McCuthcheon, HH & Pincombe, J, 2001, 'Intuition: an important tool in the practice of nursing', in *Journal of Advanced Nursing,* vol. 35, no. 5, pp. 342-348.

Meleis, AI (ed) 2007, *Theoretical nursing,* 4th edn, Lippincot, Williams and Wilkins Publishers, Philadelphia.

Melnechenko, K.L 2003, 'To make a difference: nursing presence', in *Nursing Forum,* vol. 38, no. 2, pp. 18-24.

Mezirow, J 1991,*Transformative dimensions of learning,* Jossey-Bass, San Francisco.

Mezirow, J 1994, 'Understanding transformation theory', in *Adult Education Quarterly,* vol. 44, no. 4, pp. 222-232.

Mezirow, J (ed) 2000, *Learning as transformation,* Jossey-Bass, San Francisco.

Mezirow, J 2003, 'Transformative learning as discourse', in *Journal of transformative education,* vol. 1, no. 1, pp. 58-63.

Mintz, A 1978, *George Eliot & the novel on vocation,* Harvard University Press.

Mitchell, GJ 1999, 'The view of freedom within the human becoming theory', in *Illuminations*, (ed) R. Rizzo-Parse, Jones and Bartlett Publishers, Sudbury MA.

Mok, E & Chiu, PC, 2004, 'Nurse-patient relationship in palliative care', in *Journal of Advanced Nursing*, vol. 48, no. 5, pp. 475-483.

Muncey, T 2005, 'Doing autoethnography', in *International Journal of Qualitative Methods'*, vol. 4, no. 1, pp. 2-1.

Muncey, T 2010, *Creating autoethnographies*, Sage Publications, Thousand Oaks, California.

Mykhalovskiy, E. 1997, 'Reconsidering "table talk": Critical thoughts on the relationship between sociology, autobiography and self-indulgence', in *Reflexivity and Voice*, (ed) R Hertz, Sage Publications, Thousand Oaks, London.

McAdams, DP 1993, *The stories we live by: personal myths and the making of the self*, Guilford Press, New York and London.

Newman, M 1994, *Health as expanding consciousness*, 2nd edn, Jones and Bartlet Publishers, Sudbury.

Newman, MA, Sime, MA & Corcoran-Perry, SA 1991,' The focus of the discipline of nursing', in *Advances in Nursing Science*, vol. 14, no. 1, pp. 1-6.

Newman, M, 2006, Health as Expanding Consciousness, Personal Web page, accessed 18.07.2007, http://www.healthexpandingconsciousness.org

Newman, MA 2008, *Transforming Presence*, F.A Davis Company, Philadelphia.

Nortvedt, P 1998, 'Sensitive judgment: an inquiry into the foundations of nursing ethics', in *Nursing Ethics*, vol. 5, no. 5, pp. 386-392.

Norris, JR 2002, 'One-to-one tele-apprenticeship as a means for nurses teaching and learning Parse's theory of human becoming', in *Nursing Science Quarterly*, vol. 15, no. 2, pp. 143-149.

O'Brien, ME 2001, *The Nurse's Calling*, Paulist Press, New York/ Mahwah, N.J.

O'Hara, M 2002, 'Cultivating consciousness: Carl R. Rogers's person-centered group process as transformative androgogy', in *Journal of Transformative Education*, vol.1, no. 1, pp. 64-79.

Ohlen, J & Segesten, K 1997, 'The professional identity of the nurse: concept analysis and development', in *Journal of Advanced Nursing*, vol. 28, no. 4, pp. 720-727.

Ohman, M & Soderberg, S 2004, 'District nursing – sharing an understanding of being present. Experiences of encounters with people with serious chronic illness and their close relatives in their homes', in *Journal of Clinical Nursing*, vol. 13, pp. 858-855.

Olthuis, G, Dekkers, W, Leget, C & Vogelaar, P 2006, 'The caring relationship in hospice care: an analysis based on the ethics of caring conversations', in *Nursing Ethics*, vol. 13, no. 7, pp. 29-40.

O'Rawe-Amenta, M 1986, 'Holism, hospice and nursing', in *Nursing care of the terminally ill*, (eds) M O'Rawe-Amenta & NL Bohnet, Little, Brown and Company, Boston.

O'Rawe-Amenta, M & Bohnet, NL 1986, (eds) *Nursing Care of the Terminally Ill*, Little Brown and Company, Boston, Toronto.

Osmond, J & Darlington, Y 2005, 'Reflective analysis: techniques for facilitating reflection', in *Australian Social Work*, vol. 58, no. 1, pp. 3-14.

Panke, JT 2003,' Difficulties in managing pain at the end of life', *Journal of Hospice Nursing*, vol. 5, no. 3, pp. 83-90.

Parse, RR 1981, *Man-living-health: a theory of nursing*, John Wiley and Sons Publishers, New York, Chichester, Brisbane, Toronto.

Parse, RR (ed) 1999, *Illuminations: the human becoming theory in practice and research*, Jones and Bartlett Publishers, Sudbury.

Parse, RR 2002, 'The pattern that connects', *Advances in Nursing Science*, vol. 24, no. 3, pp. 1-7.

Parse, RR 2001, *Qualitative inquiry: the path of sciencing*, Jones and Bartlett Publishers, Sudbury.

Patton, JF 2006, 'Jungian spirituality: a developmental context for late-life growth', in *American Journal of Hospice and Palliative Medicine*, vol. 23, no. 4, pp. 304-308.

Payne, N 2001, ' Occupational stressors and coping as determinants of burnout in female hospice nurses', in *Journal of Advanced Nursing*, vol.33, no. 3, pp. 396-405.

Pesut, B 2008, 'A conversation on diverse perspectives of spirituality in nursing literature', *Nursing Philosophy*, vol. 9, pp. 98-109.

Pelias, RJ 2012, 'On the joy of connections', in *Qualitative Communication Research*, vol.1, no. 2, pp.163-167.

Perry, J 2001,' Dialogical intersection: the death of a father', in *Journal of Loss and Trauma*, pp. 161-182.

Petrosino, BM 1985, 'Characteristics of hospice patients, primary caregivers and nursing care problems: foundations for future research', in *The Hospice Journal*, vol. 1, pp. 3-9.

Picard, C & Jones, D 2005, *Giving voice to what we know*, Jones and Bartlett Publishers, Sudbury, Massachusetts.

Picard, C & Mariolis, T 2002, 'Praxis as a mirroring process: teaching psychiatric nursing grounded in Newman's health as expanding consciousness', in *Nursing Science Quarterly*, vol. 15, no. 2, pp. 118-122.

Polanyi, M 1966, *The tact dimension*, New York Garden: Garden City.

Poulos, CN 2008, 'Narrative conscience and the autoethnographic adventure: probing memories, secrets, shadows, and possibilities', in *Qualitative Inquiry*, vol. 14, no. 1, pp. 46-66.

Pratt, MB 1995, 'S/HE', Alyson Books, Los Angeles.

Pullman, D 2002, 'Human dignity and the ethics and aesthetics of pain and suffering', *Theoretical Medicine*, vol. 23, pp. 75-94.

Radwin, L & Alster, K 2002, 'Individualized nursing care: an empirical definition', in *International Nursing Review*, vol. 49, pp. 54-63.

Randall, F & Downey, R.S 2006, *Philosophy of Palliative Care*, Oxford University Press, Great Clarendon Street, Oxford.

Reed- Danahay, DE (ed) 1997, *Auto-Ethnography*, Berg Publishers, Oxford, New York.

Richardson, L 1992, 'The consequences of poetic representation: writing the other: rewriting the self', in *Investigating subjectivity: research on lived experience*, (eds) C Ellis & MG Flaherty, Sage Publications, Newbury Park, London, New Delhi.

Richardson, L 1997, *Fields of play: constructing an academic life*, Rutgers University Press, New Brunswick, New Jersey.

Riggio, RE & Taylor, S 2000, 'Personality and communication skills as predictors of hospice nurse performance', in *Journal of business and psychology*, vol. 15, no. 2, pp. 351-359.

Rogers, ME 1970, *The theoretical basis of nursing*, FA Davis Company, Philadelphia.

Rosenau, PM 1992, *Post-modernism and the social sciences*, Princeton University Press, Princeton, New Jersey.

Ruth-Sahd, LA & Tisdell EJ 2007, 'The meaning and use of intuition in novice nurses: a phenomenological study', in *Adult Education Quarterly*, vol. 57, no. 2, pp. 115-140.

Ryan, JJ 1977, 'Humanistic work: Its philosophical and cultural implications', in *A matter of dignity: Inquiries into the humanization of work*, (eds) W J Heisler & JW Houck, University of Notre Dame Press, Notre Dame.

Sabatino, CJ 1999, 'Reflections on the meaning of care', in *Nursing Ethics*, vol. 6, no. 5, pp. 574-582.

Sacks, JL & Nelson, JP 2007, 'A theory of non-physical suffering and trust in hospice patients', in *Qualitative Health Research*, vol. 17, no. 5, pp. 675-689.

Salamagne, M 1997, 'Hospice in France', in *Hospice care on the international scene*, (eds) C Saunders & R Kastenbaum, Springer Publishing Company Inc., New York.

Sandgren, A, Thulesius, H, Fridlund, B, & Petersson, K, 2006, 'Striving for emotional survival in palliative cancer nursing', in *Qualitative Health Research*, vol. 16, no. 1, pp. 79-95.

Sandstrom, KL, Martin, DD & Fine, GA (eds) 2006, *Symbols, selves and social reality*, 2nd edn, Roxbury Publishing Company, Los Angeles, California.

Saunders, C & Kastenbaum, R (eds) 1997, *Hospice care on the international scene*, Springer Publishing Company.

Saunders, C 1981, 'Hospices', in *Dictionary of Medical Ethics*, (eds) AS Duncan, CR Dunstan & RB Welbourne, Longman and Todd, London.

Schneider, P 2005, 'What does it take to be a good hospice nurse', Nevada Nurses Association, viewed on 05.06.2007, http://www.proquest.com

Scott, PA 2000, 'Emotion, moral perception, and nursing practice', in *Nursing Philosophy*, vol. 1, pp. 123-133.

Shaffir, W 1999,'Doing Ethnography: reflections on finding your way', in *Journal of Contemporary Ethnography*, vol. 28, no. 6, pp. 676-686.

Sherman-Heyl, B 2002, 'Ethnographic interviewing', in *Handbook of ethnography*, (eds) P Atkinson, A Coffey, S Delamont, J Lofland & L Lofland, Sage Publications Ltd, 6 Bonhill Street, London EC2a 4PU.

Shorter, M & Stayt, LC 2009, 'Critical care nurses experience of grief in an adult intensive care unit', in *Journal of Advanced Nursing*, vol. 66, no. 1, pp. 159-167.

Smith, C 2005, 'Epistemological intimacy: a move to autoethnography', in *International Journal of Qualitative Methods,* vol. 4. no. 2, pp. 1-7.

Sorensen-Marshall, E, 2009, 'Margaret Shanks, nurse to Susan B. Anthony: exploring the extraordinary in the "ordinary" nurse', in *Advances in Nursing Science,* vol. 32, no. 1, pp. 43-54.

Sorrell, JM 1994, 'Remembrance of things past through writing: aesthetic patterns of knowing in nursing', *Advances in Nursing Science,* vol. 17, no. 1, pp. 60-70.

Spiro, H 1992, 'What is empathy and can it be taught?', in *Annals of Internal Medicine,* vol. 116, pp. 843-846.

Spry, T 2011, 'Performative autoethnograph: critical embodiments and possibilities', in *The Sage Handbook of Qualitative Research,* 4th edn, (eds) NK Denzin & Y Lincoln, Sage Publications, Thousand Oaks, California.

Stanley, KJ 2002, 'The healing power of presence', in *Oncological Nurses Forum,* vol. 29, no. 6, pp. 935-940.

Strang, P, Strang, S, Hultborn, R & Arner, S 2004, 'Existential pain an entity, a provocation, or a challenge?', in *Journal of Pain and Symptom Management,* vol. 27, no. 3, pp. 241-250.

Sundin, K & Jansson, L 2003, 'Understanding and being understood as a creative caring phenomenon in care of patients with stroke and aphasia', in *Journal of Clinical Nursing,* vol. 12, pp. 107-116.

The Ottowa Citizen, April 25, 2005, 'A moral force: the story of Dr Balfour-Mount' on line, viewed on 18.05.11, http://www.canada.com/ottawacitizen/story.html?id=896d005a-fedd-4f50-fedd-a2d9-83a95fc56464

Teilhard de Chardin, P 2012, Quotation, viewed 14 January, 2011, http://www.brainyquote.com/quotes/authors/p/pierre_teilhard_de_chardi.htm#ixzz1jO1564pp

Thiel, MM & Harris, S 2005, 'Hope and vocation', in *The Journal of Supportive Oncology,* vol. 3, no.3, pp . 234-5.

Thoresen, L 2003, 'A reflection on Cicely Saunders' views on a good death through the philosophy of Charles Taylor', in *International Journal of Palliative Nursing,* vol. 9, no. 1, pp. 19-23.

Thornburg, P, Myers-Schim, S & Grubaugh, K 2008, 'Nurses' experiences of caring while letting go', in *Journal of Hospice and Palliative Nursing,* vol. 10, no. 6, pp. 382-391.

Tillman-Healy, L 1996, 'A Secret Life in Culture of Thinness: Reflection on Body, Food and Bulimia', in *Composing ethnography* (eds) C Ellis & A Bochner, Alta Mira Press, Walnut Creek, California.

Tillman, LM 2005, 'The State of Unions; Activism (and in-activism) in Decision 2004', Conference presentation, University of Chicago, Urbana Campus, 2005.

Vachon, ML 1987, *Occupational stress in the care of the critically ill, the dying and the bereaved*, Hemisphere Publishing Corporation, New York, Washington, Philadelphia, London.

Valle, RS & King, M 1978, *Existential-phenomenological alternatives for psychology*, Oxford University Press, New York.

Van Manen, M 1990, *Researching lived experience*, The University of Western Ontario, London, Ontario Canada.

Van Manen, M 1998, 'Modalities of body experience in illness and in health', *Qualitative Health Research*, vol. 8 no. 1, pp. 1-24.

Van Manen, M 1999, 'From meaning to method', in *Qualitative Health Research*, vol. 7, no. 3, pp. 345-369.

Warren, CAB, Archer D, Broderik SC, Dobbs D, Flores RF, Grow L, Hackney J, TX Garner, Kivett D, Johnson R, Pereira-Nunez ER & Robinson C 2000, 'Writing the other, inscribing the self', in *Qualitative Sociology*, vol. 2, no. 3, pp. 183-199.

Watson, J 1999, '*Postmodern nursing and beyond*', Churchill Livingston Harcourt Brace and Company Limited, 24-28 Oval Court, London NW 1 7DX.

Watson, J 2003, 'Love and caring: ethics of face and hand – an invitation to the heart and soul of nursing and our deep humanity', in *Nursing Administration Quarterly*, vol. 27, no. 3, pp. 197-202.

Wayman, LM & Barbato-Gaydos, HL 2005, 'Self-transcending through suffering', in *Journal of Hospice and Palliative Nursing*, vol. 7, no. 5, pp. 263-270.

Waymer, D 2008, 'A man: an autoethnographic analysis of black male identity negotiation', in *Qualitative Inquiry*, vol. 14 no. 6, pp. 968-989.

WebMD on line viewed 23.5.2012, http://www.webmd.com/search/search_results/default.aspx?query=Hospice

Weisman, AD 1977, 'The psychiatrist and the inexorable', in *New meanings of death*, (ed) H Feifel, McGraw-Hill, New York.

Wengstrom, Y & Ekedahl, M 2006, 'The art of professional development and caring in cancer nursing', in *Nursing and Health Sciences,* vol. 8, pp. 20-26.

White, SJ 1997, 'Empathy: a literature review and concept analysis", *Journal of Clinical Nursing,* vol. 6, pp. 253-25

White K 2002, 'Nursing as vocation', in *Nursing Ethics,* vol. 9, no. 3, p. 279.

White, S 2003, 'Autoethnography – an appropriate Methodology', in *Qualitative Research Journal,* vol. 3, no. 2, pp. 22-32.

Wilber, K 2004, *The Simple Feeling of Being,* Shambala Publication Inc.

Wilkinson, J 1999, 'Implementing reflective practice', in *Nursing Standard,* vol. 13, no. 21, pp. 36-41.

Willis, P 1999, 'Looking for what it's really like: phenomenology in reflective practice', *Studies in Continuing Education,* vol. 21, no. 1.

Wilson, C 2005, 'Said another way: My definition of nursing', in *Nursing forum,* vol. 40, no. 3, pp. 116-118.

World Health Organisation's definition of palliative care, on line, accessed 23.5.2012, http://whqlibdoc.who./hq/2003/WHO_CDS_STB_2003.22.pdf

World Health Organisation History, Projects, Structure 2012, on line, accessed 23.5.2012, http://en.wikipedia.org/wiki/World_Health_Organisation

Wright, DJ 2001, 'Hospice nursing: the speciality', in *Cancer Nursing,* vol. 24, no. 1, pp. 20-27.

Wright, DJ 2002, 'Researching the Qualities of Hospice Nurses', in *Journal of Hospice and Palliative Nursing,* vol. 4, no. 4. pp. 210-216.

Wright, J 2008, 'Searching one's self: the autoethnography of a nurse teacher', in *Journal of research in nursing,* vol. 13, no. 4, pp. 338-347.

York, L & Sharoff, L 2001, 'An extended epistemology for fostering transformative learning in holistic nursing education and practice', in *Holistic Nursing Practice,* vol. 16, no. 1, pp. 21-29.

Young, ML 2008, 'Death comes', in *Qualitative Inquiry,* vol. 14, no. 6, pp. 990-998.

Zikorus, P 2007, 'The importance of a nurse's presence', *Holistic Nursing Practice,* vol. 21, no. 4, pp. 208-210.

Zilberfein, F & Hurwitz, E 2004, 'Clinical social practice at the end of life', in *Living with Dying*, (eds) J Berzoff & PR Silverman, Columbia University Press, New York.

Zysberg, L & Berry, MD 2005, 'Gender and students' vocational choices in entering the field of nursing', in *Nursing Outlook,* vol. 53, pp. 193-198.

Lightning Source UK Ltd.
Milton Keynes UK
UKOW04f2158220917
309708UK00001B/168/P